They Shall Be Mine

John Tallach

Illustrated by
Lawrence Littleton Evans

THE BANNER OF TRUTH TRUST

THE BANNER OF TRUTH TRUST
3 Murrayfield Road, Edinburgh EH12 6EL
P O Box 621, Carlisle, Pennsylvania 17013, USA

★

©*John Tallach* 1981
First Banner of Truth Trust edition 1981
ISBN 0 85151 320 4

★

They Shall Be Mine

Preface

The title of this book is taken from the words in the Prophecy of Malachi: 'And they shall be mine, saith the Lord, in the day when I make up my jewels' On that last day God will hold up His people, as we would hold up something very precious and show it to our friends.

But jewels have to be worked on; they have to be polished and set. And it is in this world that God prepares His jewels. In this book you can see how He worked on a few of them. Of course I should say *is working* regarding some; because, at the time of writing, they are still in the world.

Some of these stories were first published in *The Gospel Magazine*, in the section *For Younger Readers*, during the period when I was editor.

I would like to thank the publishers for their assistance and encouragement in preparing this book. Grateful thanks are also due to Mr S M Houghton and Lady Catherwood for their helpful criticisms.

Aberdeen   John Tallach
February, 1981

Contents

1
The Sister on the Hill

In the summer of 1839, four Scottish ministers were travelling across the Egyptian desert by camel. They had left home in April, and it would be a few months yet before their journey would end. They were looking for a suitable place where their church could begin a mission to the Jews.

Perhaps the heat in the desert between Egypt and Palestine was too much for Dr Black. In any case, he fell from his camel and hurt himself badly. What could they do now? Two ministers would go on, they decided, and one would go back home with Dr Black.

So Dr Black and Dr Keith sailed from Egypt to the Black Sea. There they boarded a steamer which took them up the great River Danube. It was Autumn now, the worst time to be travelling. The boat crept up the river, the sun was scorching hot, and the air was full of fever. Both the travellers became sick.

Before they had left home all had agreed that, wherever they might look for a place to begin a mission, they could forget about the Austrian Empire. The Austrian government, they were sure, would never allow them to begin a mission on their soil. But here they were, coming home by this unexpected route, passing through the heart of that Empire—surely this part of their journey was just a waste of time! At last they came in sight of Pesth, the capital of Hungary, part of the Austrian Empire. On one side of the river there was a hill and on top of the hill a huge building. Dr Keith and Dr Black asked who owned it. 'The Prince Palatine,' they were told. 'He is an uncle to the Emperor, an Austrian Archduke, and Viceroy of Hungary.'

Sick, friendless and almost hopeless, Dr Black and Dr Keith got off the steamer at Pesth and found an hotel. For the next few days they wandered about the streets, getting to know the city. A place of particular interest was the market. Here country folk arrived in the early morning, driving wagons with bread and fruit and vegetables piled high. They were in their summer clothes—wide baggy trousers and a short vest, nothing in the space between but sunburnt skin! On top they wore a bunda (a sheepskin coat), the woolly side turned out to provide protection from the heat.

As the Scotsmen toured the city, they learned that there were about 1200 Jews there. Slowly, a thought began to creep into the minds of the two ministers: 'Could it possibly be that this is the very place we are looking for?' But then they would look across the river at that huge palace, towering above the city. 'We need never think of having a mission,' one would say to the other, 'under the eye of an Austrian Archduke.'

One of these days, as Dr Keith was walking along a street in Pesth, he suddenly felt sick and weak. He had to lie down for a while, and when he was strong enough he made his way slowly back to his hotel. There he fell onto his bed, and in the hours that followed he grew weaker. Dr Black walked back and fore in the room, weeping for his friend. He felt sure that Dr Keith would die. A doctor came, but it seemed that nothing could be done. Poor Dr Black was so shocked that he became ill as well. His fever returned and he too lay prostrate in another room. The owner of the hotel became alarmed. He had two strangers under his roof, one of them very ill and the other apparently dying. He rushed out into the street and spoke to a passing Englishman. Through this man, in an extraordinary way, word of the two sick visitors reached the palace on the hill. If they had known what was happening, both Dr Black and Dr Keith would have done all in their power to prevent their presence in Pesth being known in the palace. But they were too ill to know anything. In fact, at one time Dr Keith's pulse stopped beating. It looked very like the end.

★

Maria Dorothea was a German princess, but she had come to Hungary to marry Joseph, Archduke-Palatine, Viceroy of Hungary. She felt quite alone in Hungary; it was a Roman Catholic country. She was a Protestant, and the Hungarian authorities were strongly opposed to all Protestants. Maria Dorothea was not just a Protestant in name. She really loved her Bible, and in her loneliness it became more and more precious to her. Every day she would sit with her Bible beside a window in the palace, and there she would pray to God for herself and for Hungary. Sometimes she would stand up beside the window and look out. The great River Danube rolled below, and there, on the opposite bank, stretched out the huge city of Pesth with its hundred thousand inhabitants. The thought of that city and the vast Hungarian plains stretching beyond it, without the gospel and without God, was sometimes too much for her. Turning from the window she would stretch out her arms to heaven and plead with God to send a missionary to Hungary.

This had gone on for about seven years—her loneliness, and her prayers for a missionary. Then, in the middle of one night, she suddenly awoke with the feeling that something was to happen to her. She lay awake for an hour, then went back to sleep until the morning. The next night it happened again. Maria Dorothea had never had such an experience before, and she was never to have it in the future, but the same thing happened on this occasion for night after night.

After a fortnight of this, she heard that a Christian minister had taken lodgings at an hotel in the city, and that he seemed to be dying. What was his name? 'Dr Alexander Keith,' she was told. 'But he is the man whose book on prophecy I have read,' thought the Archduchess. At once she felt sure that Dr Keith's arrival in Pesth was the event of which she had been warned.

Dr Keith stirred. The doctor who was attending him saw that he had gained a little strength, and shouted in his ear, 'We all thought you were dead'.

'Not dead,' was all Dr Keith could reply. After that he became unconscious again, and lay for days without taking notice of anybody. Then again he opened his eyes and looked around. 'What day is this?' he asked. When he was told, he said, 'Not possible'. The last day he could remember was the one ten days before.

Suddenly there was a disturbance in the street outside. A large carriage had driven up and had stopped outside the hotel. Inside

the hotel people began scurrying to and fro, preparing for the arrival of an important visitor. 'The Princess Palatine,' was hurriedly whispered all over the hotel. She who lived in the Archduke's palace had never been seen in one of Pesth's hotels before; what was bringing her now? She and her lady in waiting entered, and were shown into Dr Keith's bedroom. Her first visit lasted only moments, but it marked a great change. Anything that might help Dr Keith's recovery was done for him after that! His bed was too short, but it was replaced by the longest bed in the palace. A soldier was stationed at each end of the street to reduce the traffic and to keep any carriages which had to pass through at walking speed. The Archduchess even had straw spread on the street outside the hotel, to keep down the level of noise.

On her fourth visit, the Archduchess told her lady in waiting to stay in another room. This time, coming in to see Dr Keith alone, she was able to tell him everything. She told him of her prayers that a minister might be sent to Hungary, that she might meet someone with whom she could speak about the things which meant most to her. She told him, too, about her son, about how he had come to know the Saviour and how she had nursed him until his death two years before, only seventeen years of age. Did this mean that God was angry with her because of some sin?

Dr Keith raised himself on his elbow and gave her such a look as she would never forget. 'No, Madam,' he said, and pointed her to that verse in his French Bible which said, 'All things work together for good to them that love God'. The Archduchess could not speak English, and he could not speak German; French was the only language in which they could speak. How thankful Dr Keith now was that, when his other books had been packed up in boxes on his entry into the country, not to be opened again until he left, he had kept his French Bible out!

Dr Keith was still having attacks of fever. But they came only every second day, and on the days between the attacks the Archduchess came. The fear of fever could not keep her away, nor did she care for what other people said. One day Dr Keith heard that the city of Pesth was all excited about her visits to him. The people thought that a mission to the Roman Catholics was being set up, and they were gathering together to oppose any such thing. Spies were watching the hotel to see who came and went. The minister sent a messenger to the Archduchess, warning her that perhaps she should not come. But she came just the same, smiling as usual. To Dr Keith's anxious look she said, 'I know all they are doing, or can do. They can only lodge a complaint, to be presented to the Empress. But I have already written to her that I have seen you, and will see you, and nothing shall prevent me.'

As the weeks passed, the time came round when Dr Black would have to leave Pesth and go home to Scotland. Some time later Dr Keith also was to have left, but another attack of fever made his departure impossible. And the delay of his departure was of the greatest importance. For, by the time that Dr Keith eventually left Pesth, he had become convinced that here was the very place where God had purposed that this mission to the Jews should begin.

But how was a mission to stand up to opposition from the government? Protection was to come from that very palace which the two ministers, on their arrival, had feared most. For as soon as the Archduchess heard a whisper of Dr Keith's plans, she said that she would protect any such mission from the dangers to which it would be exposed.

On one occasion, when the Archduchess was away from Pesth, the police entered the room of one of the missionaries. The room was full of Jews, attending a gospel meeting. Seeing the Archduchess was away, the police thought they had a chance to disrupt the mission. They called one of the missionaries before a police court and ordered him to leave the city on the following Tuesday. But the Archduchess came back to Pesth on the Saturday and called the missionary to the palace. When she heard his story she solved the problem by appointing him her palace preacher. So every Lord's Day they came across from the city and walked in through the palace gates—Jews and others, rich and poor. They were going to the service held under the protection of one they had come to know as 'the sister on the hill'.

Another proof that God was working in that mission came later. Six of the Jews who had become Christians had been trained by the missionaries for two years so that, if it became possible for them to go out as missionaries into the country round about, they would be ready to go. The two-year period came to an end, and it seemed that all the training would be useless. The government was still so opposed to the mission that it appeared impossible for these Jews to begin their work.

A few days later, the Archduke was pacing restlessly up and down in one of the palace rooms. The Archduchess came into the room and asked him what was wrong. He told her the news which he had just received: there had been fighting in southern Poland (which, like Hungary, was part of the Austrian Empire) and many people had been killed. The Archduke's next statement took his wife by surprise:

'The only thing that will help these people is to circulate the Bible among them.'

Immediately the Archduchess asked, 'If this were done in Hungary, would you give it your protection?'

He answered, 'Yes, I certainly would.'

So God had made it all possible, and six converted Jews went out to the hills and plains of Hungary, seeking to bring the gospel to the other 300,000 Jews who lived there.

One development from these eventful days in Pesth concerned the Archduke. He had read the Bible for years, but Maria Dorothea's constant prayer was that her husband might come to know Jesus as his Saviour.

A few months before he died, he suddenly became ill. This illness made him feel his need to be prepared to die. As time passed he grew stronger, but for a fortnight it seemed that his mind was completely taken up with the question of whether or not he was ready to meet with God. Afterwards he told his wife that his whole life had been passing before his mind. 'Everywhere,' he said, 'I have discovered sin.' And yet the Archduke was more cheerful now; there was something giving him hope.

Soon afterwards he fell ill again, and it became clear that he was going to die. A few hours before his death the Archduchess asked him a question:

'As you are so soon to stand before the judgment seat, I wish to hear from you for the last time, What makes you hope that you are going to be with God?'

'The blood of Christ alone,' he replied. And, though his voice was weak, he placed great emphasis on the word *alone*.

★

When Dr Black fell from his camel in the Egyptian desert, neither he nor Dr Keith could have dreamt that this would lead them to the place which they had set out to find, back in the spring of that year. Nor could they have known that their arrival in Pesth, sick and friendless, was to be the answer to the prayers which the Archduchess had been offering for seven years. But Christians must expect surprises, because they serve a God who is 'able to do exceeding abundantly above all that we ask or think'.

2
Good for Evil

Long ago the Highlands of Scotland were dangerous to live in. Not that the place was inhabited by wild animals, but the people were very ignorant of the gospel. Jesus Christ was hardly known; with the result that the people lived in disobedience to God's law, fighting and quarrelling among themselves. It would take a very brave man to settle among them as a minister, seeking to lead them to the Prince of Peace.

But such a man was Aeneas Sage, who became the first minister of Lochcarron. Lochcarron is a scattered village, set beside the mountains, overlooking a large sea loch. To this Highland village came Aeneas Sage, with a few friends, in the spring of 1726. They did not get much of a welcome. The only accommodation they were offered in all the parish was a barn whose walls were made of wickerwork, interwoven between pillars of stone and turf. (They were made in this way to let the wind pass through, so that corn stacked there after being harvested could continue to dry.) It was a draughty bedroom, but the visitors made the best of it and settled down to sleep.

★

The work in the fields had stopped, the people were in their houses and the village lay in silence. Some hours of darkness passed. Then a door in one of the houses opened slowly, and a man crept out. He might have stumbled in the darkness, but he had a burning torch in his hand, lit from the dying embers of the fire in the centre of his low thatched cottage. Slowly he picked his way, the torch throwing weird shadows as the flame from it rose and fell.

At last he stood opposite the barn where he knew the minister and his friends were asleep. He stepped very carefully now, not wanting to make a sound. The light from his torch lit up the wall of the barn. He stepped close and looked at the low roof. The thatch was dry. He held his torch to the side of the barn until the flame leapt up. Quickly he moved along and held his torch against another part, and then another. In a moment or two the building was ablaze. He had waited long enough; he turned and ran.

Inside the barn the visitors were now wide awake. Nearly choking in the smoke, they set about the work of extinguishing the fire. But one of them did not seem to care about saving the barn. He leapt to the door, just in time to glimpse someone throwing away a flaming torch and running off into the dark. The man from within the barn gave chase. Perhaps there was some light from the moon by which he kept the fleeing figure in sight. The villager made a great effort to reach his home, but just before he did so a mighty hand took hold of him from behind. He struggled to escape, but soon he knew that few in Scotland could have escaped from that man's grip. He was dragged back to the scene of his crime, where the fire had now been put out.

So this was the kind of minister Lochcarron had got! He had run half-clothed through the night to catch a member of his new congregation and to call him to account. Mr Sage put his captive down in the centre of the barn floor and asked him:

'Did you set the barn on fire?'

'Yes.'

'Why did you do it?'

'To get rid of the new minister. But now I am in your hands, and you can take your revenge.'

'We'll take our revenge all right,' said Mr Sage. 'But you watch how we do it.'

Food and drink were set before the frightened man, and the minister asked a blessing on it for him. The man had expected a beating, but instead he got a hearty meal. He was hungry, he ate the meal, and when he got home he told them all about it.

Soon word went round the whole parish. The new minister was not the kind of man they had thought he would be. In a place where strength to fight was what gave a man fame, a minister had appeared who was stronger than them all! But there was another reason why Mr Sage was able to win the hearts of his enemies for his Saviour and Lord. Good for evil—that was the secret of his success!

3
The Laird of Swordale

Before Aeneas Sage went to Lochcarron, in the north-west of Scotland, a Mr Stewart was minister in another Highland village, in the north-east. There were some in Mr Stewart's congregation of Kiltearn who believed in the Saviour whom he preached. There were others who did not believe, but as they watched their minister live among them year after year, they learned to respect him for his holy life. One of this group lived quite near Mr Stewart. He owned the land on which the village of Swordale stood; that is why he had the title, *Laird of Swordale.*

The town of Dingwall lies about seven miles south of the district of Kiltearn. One day news went round Kiltearn that Mr Stewart had been hoping to preach at Dingwall, but that the people there had said that they did not want a minister like him to preach to them. They had said that they would shut the doors of their church against him; in fact, some had even said that if Mr Stewart came to preach he would be in danger of his life. Word of this came to the Laird of Swordale and he was very angry. To think that these people would treat his minister like that!

'If Mr Stewart will go to Dingwall to preach,' he said, 'I'll go with him myself. I'll see that he gets into that church.' Mr Stewart was told what the Laird of Swordale had said, and he was very glad. The Laird of Swordale was one of the strongest men in all the district!

When they got to Dingwall the church was closed and some men were guarding the door. But the big man from the country was not afraid of them. He soon got the church door opened and in he went, the minister hard on his heels. The Laird did not stop till he had got Mr Stewart safely landed in the pulpit. He then turned at the top of the pulpit stairs and said to those below, 'If any of you try to lay hands on the minister, you'll feel my strength.' There he stayed throughout the service, and when it was over he took the minister safely back to his home.

Some time after this, news again went round that country village: 'The Laird of Swordale is ill'. The minister and his wife went along to visit the invalid. After a short time Mr Stewart's wife went home, but he himself remained.

In the Laird's bedroom, the man who had made the town of Dingwall afraid of his strength lay in weakness on his bed. He was very ill. But it was not only his illness that was troubling him. He was thinking of his past life, thinking of how he had

disobeyed the word of God in many ways. The thought of it all made him feel quite weak in the sight of God.

Mr Stewart began to speak about Christ the Saviour, but the

Laird replied that there was no hope at all that God would have mercy on him.

'In all my life,' he said, 'I have never done anything but what deserved God's curse.'

'But do you not remember how you protected me one day in the church in Dingwall?' asked the minister.

'Ah yes,' the big man remembered, 'but I did that for pride in myself, and not for the glory of God.'

'That may be so, but Christ is still able to save the greatest of sinners.' Mr Stewart bowed his head and prayed for his sick friend. After a time the Laird spoke. He said that he could understand how Christ could save sinners, having died for them on the cross. But he still was not willing to trust in Christ himself. How could he receive salvation as a gift, without doing anything to save himself?

Mr Stewart prayed again, and after this a change came over the sick man. Not only did he see that Christ was willing to save a sinner like himself; he was made willing in all his weakness to trust in Christ's power to save.

The visitor prayed a third time, and now there was joy in the eyes of the dying man. Christ was near to him now, he said, and His love was wonderful. And as his weakness grew greater he felt how glorious it was to be dying in the arms of One who has everlasting strength.

When the Laird died, the minister thought how extraordinary were the things that he had witnessed in that room. Deep in thought, he turned to go. Down the stairs he went, out at the Laird's gate, and along to his own house. He was still thinking deeply when he came in at his own front door and met his wife.

'You should have stayed,' he said. 'It's not every day that you'll see what I believe I saw today.'

'What was that?' she asked.

'When I went in,' her husband replied slowly, 'I found a man still in the kingdom of sin. Then I saw him come out of the kingdom of sin and enter the kingdom of grace. At last, by the time I left, he was in the kingdom of glory.'

4
Daniel Rowland

In 1733, a new minister was appointed to preach at Llangeitho, Cardiganshire, in South Wales. He was a short man, but he was broad and strong.

He was not unknown to the people; the farm cottage with mud walls and thatched roof in which he had been born twenty years before was just down the road from Llangeitho. As a boy of three he had had a remarkable escape there. A big stone came tumbling down the chimney and crashed on to the floor, just at the spot where Daniel had been sitting some moments before. His father had been a minister too; perhaps that is why there was not enough money in the house to keep the chimney in very good repair!

In those days the people of Wales knew hardly anything about the gospel. Most of them only spoke Welsh, and Welsh Bibles were very hard to get. In any case, not many of the people could read. They worked on the farms or in the coal mines or at their weaving looms, and they were very poor. Whenever they had any time free from work, they felt that the most important thing was to enjoy themselves. But as to how they should enjoy themselves, they were not guided by the word of God. Sometimes a horse and cart, arriving at a Welsh mountain village, would get a special welcome. On the cart were what looked like casks of cheese, so what was so wonderful about that? The people knew that the visitor was a smuggler, that although he offered yellow cheese and white cheese for sale, he had no cheese at all! If they asked for 'yellow cheese' it was brandy they got; and the 'white cheese' cask was full of gin.

Apart from getting drunk, what did the people of the Welsh villages do to amuse themselves? The young people often gathered on a Saturday night and if they could get someone to play a fiddle they would dance all night until the Sabbath dawned. Then they would probably go home to sleep, but on the afternoon of the Lord's Day they would start up again. Either they danced and sang, or else they joined in some sport. To keep the Sabbath as God's Day never entered their minds.

When Daniel became minister of Llangeitho, that village in a hollow between wooded hills, he was very popular. He was just like the rest of the people. On the Lord's Day he hurried through the service as if the most important thing was to get out of the church and into the nearby inn. After that he and his friends would come back to the churchyard and start a game of football. Daniel was fast on his feet and a great footballer.

Nearly all the other ministers in Wales in 1733 were like Daniel. They were not all so good at football, but as ministers they were nearly all as useless. Like their people, they lived almost as if there were no God.

★

Not long after Daniel settled as the minister of Llangeitho, he began to hear his people speak about another minister nearby. His name was Philip Pugh, and the people spoke of him as if he were different from the other ministers they knew. Mr Pugh did not hurry through the service. He preached as if God existed, as if God was angry with those who disobeyed Him. He preached as if Christ was a real Saviour, as if people would be lost in their sins if they did not know Him. Daniel heard about what Mr Pugh was preaching. He knew that people were travelling from all around to hear what Mr Pugh had to say. It made Daniel think very hard.

In 1735 a preacher called Griffith Jones from Llanddowror came to a village near Llangeitho. Some people from Llangeitho went to hear him, and Daniel went too. When they arrived the church was full; there was only room to stand. However the visitors from Llangeitho pushed in somehow, and Daniel found himself standing just opposite the pulpit.

The service started, then Mr Jones began to preach. Suddenly he stopped. He had just seen Daniel Rowland, the short minister from Llangeitho; he was standing there as if there was no-one else so important in all the world. The preacher began to pray. He prayed just for Daniel—that God would have mercy on him, and use him to His glory yet.

Among the crowds going home to Llangeitho that night, Daniel felt very small. He knew that he was different from Mr Pugh and Mr Jones. He began to feel that they were right and he was wrong. He felt ashamed of how he had wasted his time, and even wondered if he should stop preaching. From then on the sermons preached at Llangeitho were very different. Daniel began to preach against sin. The people were shocked, and soon they were talking in the country round about of 'the crazy parson of Llangeitho'.

Some of his people who did not like the change went to Mr Pugh and complained about Daniel's new preaching. But Mr Pugh replied, 'Leave him alone. I believe that God is with him, and has a great work for him to do.' To Daniel himself Mr Pugh said, 'Preach the gospel to the people. Tell them about Christ who died to save sinners.' Around that time Daniel came

to know Jesus as his own Saviour. After that it was easier for
him to speak about Jesus to others.

★

Across the hills from Llangeitho was the village of Ystrad-ffyn.
There was a woman there from Llangeitho who had married
an Ystrad-ffyn farmer. About this time the woman went back
to Llangeitho to see her sister, and during this visit she went
out to church to hear Rowland preach. The next Lord's Day
she was back again at Llangeitho, having ridden the twenty miles
from Ystrad-ffyn that morning. Her sister was astounded, and
asked if anything was wrong.

'No.'

'Are all the children well?'

'Oh yes!'

'What's the matter then?'

'I do not know exactly. But something your crazy parson said
last Sunday has brought me. It never left me night nor day. I
have spent a miserable week and I must hear him again.' She
went to the church that day, and very often during the next
half-year she spent the Lord's Day at Llangeitho Church.

After the service one day she went up to Rowland. She asked
him to come over to Ystrad-ffyn, to preach to the people there.
He was quite surprised, but in a moment he said, 'Yes, I will
come, if the minister there will agree.' The minister agreed,
and Rowland went.

The day that the crazy parson was to come, there was great
excitement at Ystrad-ffyn. The people came crowding down to
the village church, and all eyes were looking up the road towards
Llangeitho. They were watching the highest point of the road
as it crossed over the hill into the next valley where Llangeitho
was. At last, at that point, they saw a figure on a horse appear
against the sky. It was Rowland, and the news spread along
the valley like fire.

The church was packed. There were crowds of people there that day who had never seen the inside of a church for long enough. Some of them had never heard a sermon in their lives.

There was one particular gentleman who had come to make trouble. He was used to going hunting on the Lord's Day, but when he heard that Rowland was to preach he came back early from the hunt with his friends and his dogs and rode up to the church. He made his way to the front, and got a place beside the pulpit. When Rowland began the service, this man stood up. He got up on a bench so that he was standing just beside the preacher, staring in at the pulpit. The hatred that this gentleman farmer felt towards Rowland showed in his eyes. All over his face you could see how cold and hard his heart was towards the gospel which Rowland had come to preach. He stood there and glared, hoping to put Rowland off, but Rowland went right on. When he began to preach it was as if he had not even seen that man in front of him.

Some people in the church began to feel the power of the word of God. Rowland got stronger and stronger, and soon he was preaching as if he were on fire. The iceberg, standing out of the sea of faces in front of the pulpit, began to feel uncom-

fortable. He held on for a while, but before very long he had to give in. He got down off his bench and sat with the others below the pulpit. The word of God was coming to the people of Ystrad-ffyn with almighty power. By now the iceberg, so high and mighty before, had melted right down. There he sat, his head bent down to his knees, his tears falling to the floor.

When the service was over he went up to the preacher to say 'sorry'. He asked him to his fine home and Daniel Rowland stayed there that night. Many a time after that did the farmer ride over to Llangeitho to hear the crazy parson preach.

Not only did the farmer come; a number of others in Ystrad-ffyn were soon making that difficult journey too. From there, and from other villages around as well, they crowded along the country roads leading to Llangeitho. So Rowland's congregation grew and grew.

One day, as Rowland read a part of the service in the Llangeitho church, the power of God came down. He was reading the words of the prayer addressed to the Lord Jesus: 'By thine agony and bloody sweat; by thy cross and passion; by thy precious death and burial; by thy glorious resurrection and ascension; and by the coming of the Holy Spirit, good Lord, deliver us.' The love of God, made known to men through the death of Christ, became wonderfully real that day. Some people cried out; some lost their strength and sank down to the floor. But as Rowland went on with the service God strengthened him. And as he preached, the people felt the power of the word of God.

★

Once, after the service at Llangeitho was over, some rich men who had come from the southern counties of Wales followed Rowland into his house. They wanted him to go with them to preach in their homes. They tried very hard to persuade him, but he just sat there, looking another way. Then he saw an old woman at the door of his room. She was a godly woman and he said to her, 'Why are you crying?'

'Oh my dear Rowland,' she answered, 'I want you to come and preach to the ungodly men of Llanfihangel.'

'I shall come by five o'clock next Sunday,' he said, and so he did.

Ystrad-ffyn and Llanfihangel were not the only places to which Rowland went. It was not long before he began to preach in every part of Wales. Rowland knew the careless way in which most of the ministers lived—he had lived like that himself not so long before. So the people all up and down the country did not know Christ, and Rowland felt a weight of sadness on his heart for them. He began to travel to north and south, to east and west. And where he went, with a few friends, he was often badly received. He might arrive after a long journey on his pony, and if he was given some milk from a farm it might be all he would get. He would sometimes have no more to eat than the remains of the bread and cheese he had put in his pocket that morning, and no more to drink than the water from a well.

At Tydweiliog a stone was thrown which gashed his face. He was stoned at Tal-y-bont, and at Llanilar he was again pelted with stones so that he only escaped cut and bleeding. At Pwllheli, as Rowland was preaching, some men came along carrying a drum. They were banging the drum so loudly they were nearly drowning his voice, but one of them went too far. He got a big stick, hoping that with it he could make such a noise that Rowland's voice would be completely lost. But he banged so hard that the drum broke, and Rowland was left to thunder on alone. At Aberystwyth a man swore in rage that he would shoot Rowland on the spot. He raised the gun and pulled the trigger, but the gun did not go off. On one occasion a number of enemies plotted to blow him up. They stored gunpowder underneath the spot where preacher and congregation were to stand, and laid a trail of gunpowder which would act as a fuse. But the plan was discovered before the meeting took place, so again Rowland escaped.

In spite of these dangers, Rowland was glad to go; for although he suffered in these journeys there was a growing number of people in Wales who loved the Saviour. And, as the years passed, more ministers began to preach as Rowland did. This meant that, as Rowland grew older, he was more free to stay at home.

★

Below the house where he lived at Llangeitho was a meadow. At the bottom of the meadow the River Aeron flowed, and Rowland loved to walk beside that river. If there was heavy rain, the water in the river rose and rushed along; when that happened, Rowland would sometimes come down from his house and play a game. He would throw some leaves into the water and then he would run along the bank to race them. When he had run until he was past the leaves he would turn and say to them, 'There, I beat you, though I am an old man of nearly seventy years of age'.

Sometimes on Sabbath mornings Rowland would be down by the River Aeron. He was not playing then; he was praying and thinking about the message he was to preach that day. Especially on communion Sabbaths, once a month, a great crowd would gather to Llangeitho. As the morning wore on, hundreds would appear on the skyline and make their way down to the village below. From all over Wales they had come. Perhaps they were tired and hungry, perhaps they had been persecuted by the way. They were happy to arrive and, being Welsh, they did not hide their happiness. They were singing, and down the hillside on the morning breeze their songs of praise came, making the preacher of Llangeitho look up. 'Well, here they come again,' he would say, 'bringing heaven with them.'

On such occasions the church at Llangeitho was far too small; the service was held in a field. Many thousands crowded into that field, but the most important thing to Rowland was—would God be there?

He was one time crossing over the valley to preach on the other side. The people were watching him coming, but at one point he disappeared from view. The time for the service was past, and the people wondered what had happened. They walked down the road to meet him, and found him on his knees among the trees. He was praying that God would be with him, and when he was roused to come up to the service he said to his friends, 'That was a happy meeting I had there'. He would often spend the Saturday night in prayer and tears—tears because of his unworthiness to preach, and prayers that the people would be blessed.

And when the blessing of God came down on these gatherings at Llangeitho, it was a glorious scene. The preacher's thoughts seemed to rise higher and higher as he went on. He would pause every now and then. He was receiving things from the Spirit of God hardly able to be said; and yet he was being strengthened so that he could preach it all. Tears were streaming down his happy face; the people were weeping too. What made Rowland and his people weep these tears of joy? A verse from the Bible holds the answer: 'Then were the disciples glad, when they saw the Lord'.

The Countess of Huntingdon once sent an artist to paint Daniel Rowland's picture. Rowland was not very pleased. He walked uneasily from one room to another about the house. The artist could not understand it.

'Why do you refuse?' he asked.

'Why?' exclaimed Rowland. 'I am only a lump of clay like you.' At last he was persuaded to sit to have the portrait painted, but while he sat there he kept muttering, 'Alas, alas! drawing the portrait of an old sinner! Alas, alas!'

That is why the portrait of Daniel Rowland is rather dull. He was happier thinking of Jesus than of himself.

5
A Vow Fulfilled

James Kidd was the youngest of three sons. He was born in Northern Ireland in November, 1761.

When James was only a few months old his father died, and so his earliest memories were of his mother only. Mrs Kidd did her best as a poor widow to provide for her young family; but especially she did what she could to bring them to know God. Long after the days of his childhood, James could still recite portions of the Gospel of John which his mother had then given him to memorize. He remembered also how she would question him about what he was reading, and speak to him about the Saviour, Jesus Christ.

When James was about eight years old his mother took him to a communion service held in a church at Broughshane, County Antrim. Although she was poor, somehow she managed to dress her boy in a coat of rough white wool.

James might well have been proud of that little coat as he walked into church, but soon his mind was on other things. Sitting in a pew where he had a good view of the minister, he could see all that was going on. Whoever else paid attention, there was certainly one boy in the Broughshane church that day who was all ears and eyes. He listened to the sermon. Then he saw the people of God sitting at a table covered with a white cloth, with bread and wine placed on it. They were remembering the death of their Lord.

James thought to himself: 'I wish I could come to a service like this every Sabbath. That minister who is speaking about Christ must be the happiest man in all the world . . . I wish I too could be a minister. Why should I not be? *I vow I will do my best to prepare myself to become a minister.*'

But what could young James do to keep his vow? His mother could not afford to send him to school or to buy him books. Instead he managed to borrow a few school books from a friend. At these he worked as hard as he could, getting up at dawn to study them. It was not long till he could return the books; he had learned all he could from them.

Then, in the kindness of God, James Kidd met another James who was a few years older than himself. James Ritchie was a clever boy, his relations were well off, and as a result he was able to attend the local Academy. He used to lend books to James who, when he had studied them, said the lessons back to his young tutor. Like David and Jonathan in the Bible, these boys were greatly attached to each other. It was not long, however, before the older James died, and this made James Kidd the more thankful to God for the help his friend had been able to give him while he lived.

God now used other means to help James Kidd to study. For example, a kind farmer paid for him to go for six months to the very Academy which James Ritchie had attended.

In 1784, now a young married man, James left Ireland and sailed with his wife to America. There he worked as a teacher and then set up an Academy of his own. Much of North America was wild and unexplored in those days, and there were thick dark forests where people hardly ever went. One day Kidd was travelling through a forest when he decided to leave the path and explore. He wanted to find out for himself what the wildest parts were like. Further and further he wandered from the path, the forest became thicker and darker, and soon he realized that he was hopelessly lost. Days later another traveller through these woods came on him, a helpless figure, crawling on hands and knees over the rough ground. With food, water and rest James Kidd recovered, and lived to marvel at God's kindness to him.

A little time after this he decided to move once more. He got work as an usher in the College of Pennsylvania. Later on he enrolled as a student, and supported his wife and young children by working for a printer.

Before long James Kidd began to study Hebrew. This is the language of the Jews, in which the Old Testament was written, though in your Bible it has been translated into English. Only a few months after he had caught sight of those queer letters for the first time, he was able to read through the book of Genesis in Hebrew. He thought it wonderful to read for himself the very words which God had spoken to His people in Old Testament times. He began to wish that he could own a Hebrew Bible for himself, and in fact he set his eye on a fine copy which was for sale in a Dutch bookseller's shop.

Mrs Kidd was thinking of other things, however; particularly that her husband badly needed a new suit to replace the worn and baggy one he had been wearing for years. So he put their savings in his pocket and set off for the draper's shop. But the way to the draper's shop lay past the bookseller's window. He gazed longingly through the window-pane, then at last he entered the shop. When he came out, the money for his new suit was no longer in his pocket; but he had a parcel under his arm, with a book inside. Clearly the buying of a new suit of clothes would have to be put off for a time!

When he was twenty-six years old, James Kidd returned to Britain from America. But instead of making his home in Ireland it was to Scotland that he came. You can judge how far he had progressed in studying Hebrew when I tell you that in a few years he was appointed Professor of Hebrew in the University of Aberdeen.

In those days Aberdeen was just a small city, somewhat cut off from the rest of the world. Its only stage coach connection was with Edinburgh. The coach left Aberdeen at 4 o'clock every Monday morning and deposited its passengers in Edinburgh in time for dinner the following day.

It was in Aberdeen that Mr Kidd remained for the rest of

his life. Here he taught Hebrew and other languages to young students. Here, too, he preached the gospel of Christ to all who could find seats in his packed church.

Sometimes he went to preach in other Scottish towns as well. The year after he settled in Aberdeen, he was asked to visit Greenock on the River Clyde. It was the first time that he was to preach at a service leading to the remembrance of Christ's death in the Lord's Supper. He climbed up the pulpit stairs on the Sabbath morning and sat down. Suddenly his mind flew back to the church at Broughshane, to another communion Sabbath morning when he had sat in his white coat beside his mother, to the promise he had made as an eight-year-old boy to God. He had passed through many difficult times since that far-off day, but God had brought him to this. God had helped him keep his childhood vow. Perhaps the people of Greenock did not know why the preacher that day was so full of joy and thankfulness. But you and I know why.

6
John Elias

The grandfather of John Elias was a weaver. He was very kind to John, and although John's parents did not take him to church, his grandfather made sure that he went with him. He taught

John to read the Welsh Bible, and by the time he was seven John had read through more than half of the Old Testament. Once, when he and his grandfather were at a church meeting, the preacher was late. His grandfather thought that the time should not be wasted. He pushed John into the pulpit and closed the door on him, telling him to read to the congregation from the Bible. John did what he was told. He was reading from the Sermon on the Mount when he looked round and saw the preacher standing behind him at the pulpit door. He got quite a fright, closed the Bible hurriedly and got out of the pulpit as fast as he could. As the congregation saw that ten-year-old boy scurry past the preacher down the pulpit steps, they could not know that he was yet to be one of the greatest preachers ever born in Wales.

Aber-erch lay about 75 miles to the north of Llangeitho. It was a long way for John Elias to travel to hear Daniel Rowland preach. But John had heard so much about the old preacher that, by the time he was 16, he was determined that he would soon make the journey down to Llangeitho.

Then, in October 1790, John walked into a church 4 miles from his home and heard the minister give out as his text, 'Know ye not that a prince and a great man is fallen today in Israel?' At the beginning of his sermon, the minister explained why he had chosen this text; he had just heard of Daniel Rowland's death. John hardly heard a word that was spoken after that. He wept and wept. He had heard so much about the great preacher, and now he would never hear him for himself!

But if Rowland was dead, there were other ministers alive who could still preach the gospel. John was to thank God especially that he heard a preacher called Robert Roberts. The day he heard that man speak of Christ dying for sinners, John could not but say aloud in the church, 'Thanks be to God: blessed be His name for the blood of Christ!'

★

Griffith Jones was a weaver and a preacher. He lived at a village called Ynys-y-Pandy, fourteen miles from John's home. John thought that he would like to work for Griffith Jones, as he would then be nearer to where church meetings were held. His parents agreed, so John went to live with Griffith Jones, helping him with his weaving and with the work on his land.

One day another preacher came to the house of Griffith Jones. He held a service, and after that service was over he was going to hold another meeting at which the death of Christ was to be remembered in the Lord's Supper. John was not a full member of the church, so he could not join in this second service. Griffith Jones told him, 'John, you will go to make hay in the field'.

About two hours later, Mr. Jones went out of the house and along to the field where John was. He saw at once that not much hay had been turned. He also saw that John had been crying, and asked him what was wrong.

'Oh!' John replied, 'that word broke my heart, "And those that were ready went in, and the door was shut"; you shut the door today and I was out.'

Soon after that there was to be a church meeting at a farm-house not far from Ynys-y-Pandy. John wondered if he should go to the meeting and join the church, but he was not sure what to do; he felt himself very unworthy. On the day of the meeting John was working with a servant girl in a corn field; it was harvest time. When dinner time came, John did not come from the field. The servant girl told Mr Jones that she was worried about John. He would sometimes stand still, as if deep in thought. Then he would go at his work with all his might. Then he would stop again and begin to cry; sometimes he would go behind a hedge and from the groans that he made she thought he was going to die. The girl did not know what was wrong, but Mr Jones just said to her, 'Good will come of all this'.

After dinner, Griffith Jones and his wife set out for the meeting at the farmhouse. They walked past the field where John was working at the corn and they stopped to speak to him.

'We are going to the meeting,' they said. 'You do what you think is right.' The servant girl watched what happened then. After Mr and Mrs Jones had walked away, John came out of the field and began to follow them. He nearly caught up with them, but then he stopped beside a hedge. That went on for as long as the girl could see. It seemed that John wanted to walk with the other two, but when he came near he seemed afraid of joining them.

In the end, however, John's desire to join the people of God overcame his fear. He went to the meeting, the preachers asked him questions and he answered them. So John became a member of the church, and sat at the Lord's Table along with the others who believed in Jesus.

One day Mr Jones was in his workshop when he noticed a piece of paper stuffed into a hole in the wall. He pulled it out, uncrumpled it, and found some writing on it. He could just make out rough jottings—they were notes someone had scribbled down when thinking about a text of Scripture. He found quite a few bits of paper after that first one. What did it mean? It meant that, when John Elias was weaving in Mr Jones' workshop, he would sometimes be so struck by words from the Bible that he would get a piece of paper somewhere and write down his thoughts. Then he would hide away these scraps of paper, pushing them into holes in the workshop wall. As Mr Jones no doubt knew, it also meant that John was thinking about preaching the gospel. It was not long before he was being asked, not only to pray at the little church meetings held nearby, but sometimes to say a few words of his own to the people, too.

William Dafydd, an old man who had been preaching for forty years before John began, asked John to go with him when he

went out to preach. He would ask John to begin the service
for him, and sometimes he would ask John to preach. Some
people thought that John, at twenty years of age, was too young
to preach. But old Mr. Dafydd would answer them, 'When I
am in the dust this young lad will be a great man'.

His grandfather had taught him a lot, but John had never
been to school. When he began to preach he felt that he should
go somewhere to study for a while. He knew of a school run
by a minister called Evan Richardson. To that school John went,
and for some months he was able to study Greek and Hebrew.
He also studied English, because he could not speak it yet. Even
in a short time, he learned enough to be able to read English
books. For the rest of his life John was always studying; he
learned something about nearly every subject which would help
him in his preaching.

While he was studying, Elias was sometimes asked by Mr Richardson to preach. After Elias had preached one night, two boys
of seven or eight years were walking home together. One said
to the other, 'Why does John Elias stretch out his arm like that
as he preaches?'

The other boy replied, 'Oh! it is to point out the way to
heaven'.

'Does he know the road there?' asked the first boy.

'Yes,' the second replied again, 'and all the people say he
knows it very well.'

★

Since the days of Daniel Rowland, the gospel had become better
known throughout Wales. But there was a large island off the
north-west coast of the country which had hardly changed at
all. The people of Anglesey still seemed to live like heathens.
They stole, they got drunk, they quarrelled and fought. And
when a ship would founder off the Anglesey coast, many people
did not care about the lives of those who were in the boat. All

they were concerned about, as they made their way to the beach, was how much of the cargo they could carry away from the wreck.

In 1799 Elias left his native county of Caernarvonshire, crossed the Menai Strait, and settled in Anglesey. Soon he was travelling all round the island, preaching. Sometimes he preached in churches: but often he preached beside the road, on a hillside, or beside the sea. After a time a change came over the life of Anglesey. Some who had stolen from shipwrecks even carried the stolen goods back down to the shore.

Llanfechell was the name of a village near the north coast of Anglesey. On one side of an open space in that village was a shop which sold clothes and other things. Above the shop was the name of the owner, *Elizabeth Broadhead.* As Elias travelled round Anglesey he came to Llanfechell, met Elizabeth Broadhead, and they fell in love. Elizabeth's father was a wealthy man, and did not approve of her marrying someone as poor as Elias was. However Elizabeth knew what she wanted to do, and the wedding went ahead.

They were very happy together, but in the first years of their marriage the shop did not do well. Both Elias and his wife had often to pray that God would help them. Especially Elias prayed that he would not owe money to anybody. God heard their prayers, and afterwards the business prospered quite well. So from his own experience Elias could tell others to pray to God for help, whatever trouble they were in.

Across the Menai Strait from Anglesey, on the mainland of North Wales, was a town called Rhuddlan. It was the custom for many years to hold a fair outside this town at harvest time. At Rhuddlan Fair farmers would hire labourers, and all kinds of things would be sold for work on the land. The fair was held on the Lord's Day, and crowds of people came from quite a distance to attend.

In the public houses of Rhuddlan there was music and singing
and the law of God was broken in many ways.

John Elias used to hear about Rhuddlan Fair as he went about
preaching in that part of Wales. He felt sorry that people should
be so disobedient to God, and one year he decided to go himself
to the fair. He took with him a number of people who would
pray for the help of God in what they were going to do.

They arrived at the fair in the afternoon—just when it was
at its busiest. Elias and his followers made their way through
the crowds to a public house called the New Inn. There were
three steps up to the front door of the New Inn, and John climbed
them, turned, and looked around. The streets were crowded
with people, many carrying scythes or sickles which they had
just bought. Men were shouting to one another, some were playing fiddles and others were dancing to the music.

For a moment there was a lull in the noise. Many looked
towards the tall, thin figure standing at the front of the New
Inn. They were struck by his appearance; his dark hair, his open
face, his grey shining eyes. Elias told his followers to start singing
part of Psalm 24. He had with him a great singer, John Roberts;
he started the singing and the rest joined in. That singing had
a strange effect. It was not just the music; these people were
really singing the praises of God! Hundreds of people heard
it, and came close to the New Inn to see what was going on.
Soon the crowd grew to thousands. When the singing stopped
there was already a change. Some people began to hide what
they had just bought at the Fair. Then Elias read some verses
of the Bible, and when he had finished he began to pray. The
people were quite astounded. Here was a young man, standing
on the doorstep of the New Inn at the height of Rhuddlan Fair,
and he was praying to God! Silence crept over the crowd, and
as they saw the tears streaming down the face of that young
minister, they began to feel ashamed. There was another singing,

and then Elias read, in a strong clear voice, the words from
the book of Exodus: 'Six days shalt thou work, but on the seventh
day thou shalt rest; in earing time and in harvest thou shalt
rest'. The people who were with Elias were praying that God
would help him preach. And so He did. Elias spoke that day
as one sent with a message from God to Rhuddlan Fair. His
hearers became more and more afraid. They knew that they
had done wrong to break God's Day, and many cried when Elias

shouted out, 'O robbers! robbers! you are robbing the Lord; you are robbing my God of His day!'

When Elias finished preaching that summer afternoon in 1802, that was the end of the fair. There never was another Rhuddlan Fair.

★

Till about the middle of last century, Elias preached in different parts of Wales. There was no preacher like him. Perhaps others were thinking more about themselves, perhaps they were wondering what their hearers thought of them. But Elias seemed to be thinking only of God when he preached; people felt as if it was God Himself who was speaking to them. And many were converted through his preaching; they came to know for themselves the Saviour whom Elias preached.

In the study where Elias prepared his sermons, the carpet became quite worn beside his chair. It was worn because he was so often kneeling on it. And the seat was often wet because, when he prayed, he wept. He prayed because he knew that, when he went out to preach, he needed the help of God. He wept as he prayed because he felt that need so much.

Elias was preaching at meetings in 1840 when he became unwell. His trouble gradually got worse until he was not able to leave home. Many people hoped that he would preach again, but Elias knew that he never would. He thought of all the journeys he had made to different parts of Wales to preach the gospel, and now he would not be able even to leave that room!

But he was not unhappy. The same God as had been with him in his journeys was with him still, when he could no longer go. He had pain in his body, but his soul was so filled with joy that he once thought himself in heaven. If he was so happy before he arrived, how great must his joy have been when Christ welcomed him in!

[45]

7
Henry Venn

The cricket match between Surrey and All England in 1749 drew many supporters. The crowd got very excited as the match went on, but then at the end something happened which caused a lot of surprise. One of the best players, whose side had just won the match, threw his bat down on the ground.

'Whoever wants a bat which has served me well can take that one,' he said. His friends looked at him.

'Why are you giving up cricket, Henry?' they asked.

'Because I am to be ordained on Sunday,' Henry replied, 'and I will never have it said of me, "Well struck, parson".'

Many begged him to change his mind, but Henry Venn refused. From that time he gave his whole attention to his work as minister at Horsley. He preached, he gave out tracts, he spoke to people, he read a great deal. But after a time he began to doubt whether he was living as he should. According to his own ideas, he seemed to be doing quite well; but was he living to the glory of God? As the months, and then the years passed by, Henry Venn thought about that question more and more.

After four years at Horsley, Henry Venn went to Clapham in London. He was very busy, preaching in different churches in the city. Then, in 1756, he became so ill that he could not preach for eight months.

It gave him time to think. More deeply than ever before he felt one thing. It was not what he did that would count for his

salvation; it was what God would do. It was not his good living
that would save his soul, but only the mercy of God through
Jesus Christ. After that there was a change in Venn's sermons.
Now he preached more clearly than before that salvation is in
Jesus Christ alone.

★

Three years after that illness Henry was on the move again.
He and his wife left London, going north to Yorkshire. Here
he settled as minister of the large town of Huddersfield.

Most of the people of Huddersfield were very poor. They
worked at weaving looms or perhaps in the coal mines which
lay outside the town. They worked for very long hours, and
they got hardly any pay. Few of the poor children went to school
to learn to read and write. They were often hungry and they
lived in dirty homes. Nobody seemed to care.

But when Henry Venn became their minister in 1759 the people of Huddersfield began to feel that somebody loved them.
He preached on the Lord's Day in the church, and during the
week he went all around his parish. He visited the grimy villages
on the outskirts of the town, and soon he was holding eight
or ten services in houses during each week.

Venn was not long in Huddersfield when some men in a nearby
town heard about him. These men laughed at the kind of beliefs
which Venn held, and one day two of them came to Huddersfield
church to hear him preach. They were not coming to worship
God. They just wanted to hear what Venn had to say, so that
they could go back and have a good laugh about it with their
friends.

When they came near the church, however, they noticed that
things were not the same as in other churches which they had
visited. There were great crowds of people pushing into the
church, and when Venn began to preach the people felt that
what he said was true. As the service ended and the two men

left the church one of them said, 'Surely God is in this place. There is nothing to laugh about here.'

He found out where the minister was, and went to speak to him. He told him he had come to make fun of his message, and asked Venn to forgive him and to pray for him. To the end of his life this man was Venn's close friend.

The people in Venn's congregation began to feel very concerned about the things which their minister preached to them. Many, who before had known nothing about these things, began to feel that they were sinners and that they must come to know Christ as their Saviour.

One night a group of these people were praying in Huddersfield church. A boy and his uncle were passing and stopped to listen at the door. The boy, whose name was William, was sixteen years old; his uncle was nineteen. When they heard the prayers from inside the church they felt that these people must believe very deeply in what they were praying for.

Because of what they had heard, these two came back on a Thursday night to attend another service. The church was full of people. But the crowd was very quiet, except that some people were in tears. Venn's text that night was from the book of Daniel, 'Thou art weighed in the balances and art found wanting'.

William and his uncle listened very carefully, and when the service was over they went out of the church without saying a word. Silently they walked home through the fields, until the uncle stopped, leaned against a wall and began to cry. William looked at him.

'I can't stand this,' his uncle was saying as he wept. That was the night when he first realised that he was a sinner. After that Thursday night he was completely changed. William, too, was never the same after that meeting. He saw his need of a Saviour and he could not rest until he found him.

Longwood, where William lived, was three miles from Hud-

dersfield. Crowds of people used to walk from Longwood to Huddersfield church to hear Mr Venn. When they came out, they would walk along the road to Longwood together, until they came to Fir's End. There, a mile from Longwood, they would stop and talk about the sermon for a while before they separated to go to their homes. William, as an old man, never forgot standing in that crowd and listening to these discussions. Neither did he forget the minister whom he came to love, the stern look on his face as he spoke of sin and the loving look and the tears he would shed as he would speak about Jesus Christ.

★

Venn was twelve years in Huddersfield. Then, in 1771, he had to leave. He was only forty-seven years old, but he had worked so hard that he had made himself ill. He went away to Yelling, a quieter place. There he could still preach, but he did not have so much to do.

While Venn was at Yelling, one of his daughters married a man whose wife had died, leaving young children without a mother. Venn was very interested in these children to whom his daughter was now to be a mother. One of them, called John, was only three years old.

Venn asked John to come to stay at Yelling with him. When he arrived, Venn soon found out that John was very frightened of the dark. When night time came 'Venn took the little boy by the hand and led him into his study, where the shutters were already closed. The study was dark, but Venn set John on his knee, and told him such an interesting Bible story that the darkness was soon forgotten. Each night he did the same, till John looked forward every day to the evening when he went into Grandpa's study to hear a story. After Venn had told many stories with John sitting on his knee he placed John beside him in the study, still holding his hand. The next night he put him on a seat beside him, but did not hold his hand. After that he put John's seat a little distance away, and gradually he got John to listen to his story sitting in the dark, at the opposite end of the room. After that winter had passed, John was never afraid of the dark again.

For some years after John grew up, he did not care about the God of whom Henry Venn had told him. But when Henry Venn died in 1797, John thought about his 'grandfather' a great deal. Especially he recalled the last words he had heard from him, years before: 'Remember, little John, if anything could make heaven not heaven to me, it would be not having you with me there.'

After that there came a change in John's heart and life. He came to believe in Jesus, and to serve Him as his 'grandfather' had done. And when the time came for John himself to die, he would often say, 'When I get to heaven, how I shall bless God for the early lessons of dear old Henry Venn!'

8

A Dangerous Journey

John G Paton was a missionary to people who lived in some islands of the Pacific Ocean. Tanna is one of the smallest of these islands, and it was to Tanna that Paton went in 1858. He was not the only missionary on the island; a Mr and Mrs Mathieson were there too.

One day a message came to Mr Paton from Mr and Mrs Mathieson. It said that they had run short of suitable food. Paton wanted to take them food, but how could it be done? His friends lived on the other side of Tanna, and between them were groups of tribesmen who were fighting among themselves. So he could not go by land. Could he go by sea? It seemed as angry as the inland tribesmen. The waves were roaring in one after the other, dashing themselves against the shore.

But Paton was determined to go, so he asked two friendly chiefs to select their best canoe and a number of strong men.

Soon they pushed off, with Paton watching over a pot of flour tied down in the middle of the boat. Behind him was a man who, in turn, was watching Paton. For the missionary could not swim, and if the boat capsized this man was to help him to the shore. Around the coast they went, keeping just outside where the sea was breaking on the coral reef. The men paddled, and Paton prayed.

At last they came to a spot two miles from their destination, where friends of the crewmen lived. Here the men said that they were tired, that they would go no further, that this was the place where they must land.

'But it is too dangerous!' Paton protested. 'The canoe will be smashed to pieces on the reef. We must go on!' But the men wanted to visit their friends; they would not go on. They just sat there, watching the waves sweep in from the wide ocean, passing the canoe and breaking into spray and foam on the reef. Suddenly the captain shouted, 'Missi, hold on! There is a smaller wave coming; we'll ride in now.' As the wave rolled in behind them, every man dug his paddle into the sea. The canoe rose like a bird and flew in on the crest of the wave. In a moment

all was confusion. Some were swimming towards the shore, while Paton let go his hold of the boat and sprang for the reef. He had almost been swamped by the next wave when a man reached him and half carried him, half swam with him, to the shore. Through all this, one brave chief kept a hold of the boat. And when another man emerged from the boiling waters he had the pot of flour securely on his head!

When Paton had stayed a few hours with the Mathiesons, he told them he would have to go home. He was afraid that some local people would rob his house if he stayed away too long. His crew were with their friends, waiting for suitable weather before returning home. He would have to go back overland. The sun was going down; the warring tribesmen would not see him in the dark. He tried to hire men to go with him, but they refused. 'You will certainly be killed,' they said.

Praying to God for protection, he began his journey home. He followed the edge of the sea, and went as fast as he could. Darkness fell, but still he kept walking on. Then he missed his way, and after a time he began to hear voices. He peered through the bush, and saw the night fires of one of the most warlike villages. Now he knew where he was, and slowly he crept back towards the sea.

But now he faced another difficulty. To get back to the shore he had to climb down a high, steep cliff. There was a path down the cliff face, but in the dark he could not find it. He knew there was a part of the cliff which was steep but smooth. He made his way to that spot and said to himself, 'If I slide down here and the tide is far in, I will drown. But if I stay here till the morning, the savages will find me and kill me.'

He groped around for some stones, and threw them down. He hoped that by the sound they made he would know if the sea at the foot of the cliff was deep or not. But the distance was so far that the stones sent back no answer to his question.

He then took his umbrella and threw it down. Still there was no response.

He could wait no longer. Tying his clothes tightly about him, he lay on his back on the face of the rock. He lowered himself as far as the branch he was holding would reach. Then, with a cry to his Saviour to care for him, he let the branch go.

It seemed as if he were flying through the air; as if his fall would never come to an end. Then suddenly, with a tremendous splash, he hit the sea. It was deep enough to break his fall, but not so deep that he could not wade to the shore. He even found his umbrella again in the water!

When he got home, after fifteen dark and dangerous miles, his neighbours were amazed.

'Surely any of us would have been killed!' they exclaimed. 'Your God alone thus protects you and brings you safely home!'

'Yes,' replied Paton. 'And He will be your protector and helper too, if only you obey and trust in Him.'

9
Abraham

The last story told of a dangerous journey which John G Paton had to make from one side of Tanna to the other, and of how God marvellously brought him back in safety to his home.

After Paton had lived for a time in that house by the sea, he began to realize that it was not a healthy spot. He had become ill with fever fourteen times, and now he saw that he should move to higher ground. This is the point at which we first meet Abraham. He had come from the island nearby called Aneityum. He was one of the few Christian people of these South Sea islands and he had come with 'Missi Paton' to help him teach the Tannese.

Paton was ill, and as he struggled up the hill on which he wished to build, Abraham and his wife watched over him. About two-thirds of the way to the top, the missionary fell to the ground. Abraham and his wife stooped over him, and made him comfortable. Paton felt so weak that he thought death must be near, but after a little rest he began to revive. Abraham and his wife Nafatu then carried him to the top. There they gave him cocoanut juice and fed him with local food. Together with the healthy breezes which blew along the hill-top, this saved the missionary's life.

When Paton grew stronger he set about building a house on this healthier spot. But who would help him carry the planks he had bought up that steep hill? Abraham would do it: Abraham, the converted cannibal: he would help Missi Paton build a house from which he could teach the Tannese about the Saviour of the lost world.

★

Measles is an illness which nowadays can be treated fairly easily; but in Paton's time, among the South Sea Islanders, it was a deadly disease. Suddenly it struck Tanna, and many of the people died. Thirteen of those who had come from Aneityum died, and the others wanted to go home. A ship called just at that time and they all prepared to leave. Thinking that Paton was going to leave as well, Abraham packed his possessions and waited with the rest to board the boat that would take him back to his native Aneityum. Then he saw the missionary come up to him, and he got a surprise. Missi Paton was not going to leave the death-ridden island after all! When he knew that, he asked, 'Missi, would you like me to remain with you, seeing my wife is now dead and her grave is here?'

'Yes,' Paton replied, 'but considering the circumstances in which we will be left alone, I cannot plead with you to do so.'

'Then, Missi, I remain with you of my own free choice,' said Abraham. 'We will live and die together in the work of the Lord. I will never leave you while you are spared on Tanna.' The others left, but Abraham shouldered his box, picked up his bundle, and went back to his Tannese hut.

Abraham's love to Missi, and to Missi's Master, was soon to be tested. On Erromanga, an island to the north of Tanna, where a Mr and Mrs Gordon were missionaries, unrest began to spread.

The people of the island were stirred up against the missionaries by white traders who did not wish the missionaries to be there. The upshot was that Mr and Mrs Gordon were murdered.

Waves of unrest began to reach Tanna too. The more heathen among the Tannese began to say, 'How is it that Jehovah did not protect the Gordons? If the Erromangans are not punished, neither will our Tannese be punished, though they murder all Jehovah's people.' Some Tannese tried to drive Abraham and Paton apart, saying to Abraham that he should return to Aneityum, or he would certainly be killed. But Abraham replied, 'I will not leave Missi'. During these dark days Abraham and Paton were inseparable. On the evening that the Tannese had tried to frighten him away, as he was having worship with Paton, Abraham prayed:

O Lord, our Heavenly Father, they have murdered thy servants on Erromanga. They have banished the Aneityumese from dark Tanna. And now they want to kill Missi Paton and me! Our great King, protect us, and make their hearts soft and sweet to thy worship. Or, if they are permitted to kill us, do not thou hate us, but wash us in the blood of thy dear Son Jesus Christ. He came down to earth and shed his blood for sinners; through Him forgive us our sins and take us to Heaven—that good place where Missi Gordon the man and Missi Gordon the woman and all thy dear servants now are singing thy praise and seeing thy face. Our Lord, our hearts are pained just now, and we weep over the death of thy dear servants; but make our hearts good and strong for thy cause, and take thou away all our fears. Make us two and all thy servants strong for thee and for thy worship; and if they kill us two, let us die together in thy good work, like thy servants Missi Gordon the man and Missi Gordon the woman.

These were days of constant threatening. Life was uncertain; death seemed sure.

One day Paton's house was broken into, and all his valuables plundered. The day afterwards Nowar, the chief in the area where Paton lived, declared that the missionary should not wait another night near his wrecked home. He should go at once inland, and hide in a particular tree in the chief's own plantation. The chief sent his son to guide Paton to the spot. Into the branches of the chestnut tree the exhausted missionary climbed to wait and to watch. The first hours of darkness passed slowly; the night air was filled with the noise of gunfire and the yelling of savages. Yet in all his after years Paton had the most precious memories of that tree, for there he felt His Saviour nearer to him than ever before.

The moon rose. Then, about midnight, he heard a sound and saw a dark figure stand in the shadows at the foot of the tree. It was Nowar's son again, come to guide him to the sea. They walked with care, and after a time they came out of the bush to stand on a beautiful beach whose sand shone white in the moonlight.

It was time to leave Tanna, for many of the people were awaiting an opportunity to kill the missionary. Mr and Mrs Mathieson, too, were being threatened; they would all have to leave Tanna together. The gospel would return to Tanna at a later date, but for the moment the work of the missionaries there was done.

Who was to go with Paton on his canoe journey round to Mathieson's station? Abraham, he would go. Abraham would sit at the front, Paton next to him, another Aneityumese behind, the boy with the steering paddle at the end. At last they were free to go, and the canoe slid away from the shore. For an hour or so everything went well, but when they rounded a point and began to head south the wind met them with its full force. The waves rose in the darkness and dashed against the canoe. The boy in the stern stood up and cried that they would be swamped. Even Abraham at the front threw down his paddle with the rest and said, 'Missi, we are all drowned now! We are food for the sharks. We might as well be eaten by the Tannese as by fishes, but God will give us life with Jesus in heaven!'

Paton shouted to them all to be calm. He spoke to Abraham especially, demanding where his faith was now.

'Thank you for that, Missi,' Abraham said. 'I will be strong. I pray to God and ply my paddle. God will save us.' Paton had already seized the paddle nearest him, and the two of them dug their paddles into the sea. Struggling against wind and tide, they at last succeeded in turning the canoe. For the next four hours or so they fought to inch their boat round that headland, back into sheltered water. Dawn was brightening the sky as they beached again at the exact spot they had left five hours before.

Paton and his friends could do nothing now but set off overland to the other mission station. They were in constant danger, but at every step they were kept by the power of God. At one point a host of armed savages swept down on them and a killing stone was thrown at Abraham. But it whistled past him, only leaving a graze on his cheek. At another stage Paton failed to jump across a stream. As he fell, a killing stone crashed into a tree beside him, passing where his head had been a second before.

And so Abraham, who had stayed on Tanna and stuck by Missi there to the last, returned to his native Aneityum. He who had given himself to the service of Missi's Master and who had willingly accepted a life of suffering and uncertainty for love of Him, died at last peacefully at home. Paton, calling at Aneityum at a later date, was given back a silver watch which he himself had sent to Abraham from Sydney. The converted cannibal's dying wish had been: 'Give it to Missi, my own Missi Paton; and tell him that I go to Jesus, where time is dead.'

10

Rain from Below

You have now heard about Abraham, and of how he and Paton had to leave Tanna because the people were set on killing them. Paton never went back to work on Tanna again; though other missionaries did, and their work was blessed by God.

It was on Aniwa that Paton next settled. On this island, to the north-east of Tanna, he lived and worked for fifteen years. The fact that he and his helpers came at all amazed the people there. They knew how he had been treated on Tanna, just twenty miles away, and they could not understand why he stayed in the islands. One thing they knew. The missionary was not there to make money or any such thing. He had come to carry on his work of preaching the gospel. The love of God was so clearly seen in the lives of His servants that the hearts of the people were moved and they were ready to hear the message that Paton brought to them.

★

Because Aniwa is a flat island, it does not get much rain. And because it is made up almost completely of a kind of rock in which there are little holes, the rain which does fall sinks quickly out of sight, leaving the island almost as dry as before. If it were not for a certain dampness in the air, and for the heavy dews, Aniwa could hardly grow a blade of grass.

There were no wells or springs or streams on Aniwa. The people must have got used to drinking very little. What fluid they did take was mostly provided by cocoa-nuts. There was a water hole near the village beside Paton's house. But this hole, which held water for a short time after rain fell, was situated in the ground of two evil men. These men pretended to have the power to fill the hole with water, and the poor people came to pay them when the hole went dry.

Paton and the others with him felt the lack of fresh water very much. They also did not like to think how the Aniwans were kept in fear of these so-called Sacred Men, believing that they had power to make their water-hole fill up. One morning Paton announced to Chief Namakei, who had begun to show an interest in the gospel, 'I am going to sink a deep well down into the earth, to see if our God will send us fresh water up from below'.

The old Chief was very sorry to think that here, in Paton's plan, was the first sign of the missionary going mad. 'O Missi!' he pleaded, 'Wait till the rain comes down, and we will save all we possibly can for you. Rain comes only from above. How could you expect our island to send up showers of rain from below? O Missi! Your head is going wrong. You are losing something, or you would not talk wild like that! Don't let our people hear you talking about going down into the earth for rain, or they will never listen to your words or believe you again.'

But Paton would not give up his plan. He explained to Namakei that, if no fresh water could be found on Aniwa, he and his helpers might have to leave the island. Praying to God for guidance he took a pick, a spade and a bucket, selected a spot beside the road near the mission, and began to dig. He did not know very much about sinking a well, but with every blow of his pick he sent up a prayer to God.

Old Namakei was fussing about, staring at the missionary turned water engineer, and muttering, 'Poor Missi! That's the way with all who go mad. There's no driving of a notion out of their heads. We must just watch him now. He will find it harder to work with pick and spade than with his pen. When he's tired we'll persuade him to give it up.'

The old Chief was right on one point: the missionary soon got tired. But he was wrong on the other: Paton would not give up. He held up some fishhooks before the watching natives, and promised one to every man who shifted three bucketfulls of earth out of the hole.

The work went on for days. One evening, as Paton walked home after a hard day's work, he thought to himself: 'I am getting a bit low on fishhooks, but at least the hole is now twelve feet deep'. It was a comforting thought to take to bed with him that night. But next morning a shock was awaiting him. One side of the shaft had given way; the hole was as good as filled in again.

After that, there wasn't another man on Aniwa who would go down the shaft. Paton had to go on alone, doing all the picking and shovelling by himself. But then he thought of a way by which the people could help. He fitted up a beam across the mouth of the shaft and passed a rope over the beam. Then he tied his largest bucket to the bottom end of the rope, and got some men to take hold of the upper end. Paton worked inside the hole, filling up the bucket with earth, and when he

had filled it up he rang a little bell. This was the signal to the men at the mouth of the shaft to start pulling the rope. As they moved away from the shaft the bucket came up, and when it appeared at the top one man tipped out the earth: then the bucket was let down the shaft again.

He got down to a depth of twenty feet, twenty-five feet, thirty feet: still he found no water. But he kept slaving on, and then he noticed a change. The earth and coral rock were not now dry but damp.

He said to the Chief in the evening, 'I think that Jehovah God will give us water tomorrow from that hole'. Namakei seized the chance to reason again with the mad missionary. He thought that, if Paton came to water at all, it would be the sea. This would mean that he had reached the bottom of the island, upon which he could easily fall through the hole he had made into the sea and be eaten by sharks! But Paton believed that God was leading him to expect fresh water the following day, and said so.

At dawn he was at work again. At the bottom of his shaft he dug a narrow hole about two feet deep. It was not very long before he saw, trickling into the bottom of that hole, what he had come down thirty-two feet to find.

What was going on down that shaft? The men at the top began to look at one another in wonder. Surely now Missi had really gone mad! He seemed to have fallen on his knees away down there, and he was shouting excitedly. Ah! now he was starting to climb up the ladder. But what did he hold in his hand?

A jug. A jug he had taken down empty in the sight of all, and now brought it back with something in it. They crowded round and stared. Could it be water? Old Namakei took the jug in his dark hands and shook it. Whatever was inside, it *looked* like water. He put his finger in. It *felt* like water. Then the final test. He plucked up all his courage and put the jug to his lips.

The stuff in the jug ran into his mouth. He made it go round and round his mouth and finally he swallowed it. 'Rain! Rain! Yes, it is rain!'

Now all the men were as frightened as mice. They did not understand how rain could come up through the earth, and they would not go near the hole. Then after a while they formed a line, all joining hands, leading away from the hole. The man who was nearest the edge took a quick peep and then passed back to the rear. The next man, held by his neighbour, then looked down the shaft and saw the wonderful sight. They who had only seen water come from the sky were quite confused. 'The world is turned upside down,' they said.

But after a time they got used to the idea. Not only did they help Missi Paton to line the sides of the deep well with coral blocks; they also set about sinking shafts themselves in different parts of the island. But though the six or seven sites seemed perfectly suitable, not one hole led to a well. In every case, the people came against solid rock, or the water they found was salt. Then they learned what was one of the lessons of Missi's well: 'Missi not only used pick and spade, but he prayed and cried to his God. We have learned to dig, but not how to pray, and therefore Jehovah will not give us rain from below!'

And there was something else which engraved the sinking of the well on the minds of the people of Aniwa. The old Chief, who had thought that Paton was going out of his mind when he started to sink the well, said after it was finished, 'Missi, I think I could help you next Sabbath. Will you let me preach a sermon on the well?'

It was a surprising offer, but Paton accepted it. When the Lord's Day came, a great crowd of islanders came together in expectation of hearing their old Chief preach. Paton began the service, then looked over to Namakei. The Chief leapt to his feet. Dressed in a shirt and a kilt, he made a colourful figure.

Armed with a tomahawk, he was ready to enforce his message with emphatic gestures.

'Friends of Namakei,' he began, 'men, women, and children of Aniwa, listen to my words.' He went on to confess before his people how that, when Missi had come to Aniwa and told them of many things, they had not believed his words. But most of all they had laughed when Missi had spoken of digging in the earth for rain. There was a nodding of heads. His voice rose:

'We mocked at him; but the water was there all the same.' They had not believed that the rain was there: but with the help of God Missi had drawn it out. The tomahawk was swishing through the air, the crushed coral covering the floor was flying in every direction. Now this liveliest of preachers came to the point of his message. He beat his chest and exclaimed:

'Something here in my heart tells me that the Jehovah God does exist, the Invisible One, whom we never heard of nor saw till the Missi brought Him to our knowledge. The coral has been removed, the land has been cleared away, and lo! the water rises. Invisible till this day, yet all the same it was there, though our eyes were too weak. So I, your Chief, do now firmly believe that when I die, when the bits of coral and the heaps of dust are removed which now blind my old eyes, I shall then see the Invisible Jehovah God with my soul, as Missi tells me, not less surely than I have seen the rain from the earth below.'

He challenged the people to fetch their idols and cast them at the missionary's feet. Then his voice rang out with the thrilling words: 'Namakei stands up for Jehovah!'

The people listened in astonishment. They had come to hear their old Chief preach and he had certainly not let them down. They had witnessed a wonderful scene, though no one realized at the time just how wonderful that day had been. For the blessing of God was resting on the successful sinking of the well in answer to Missi's prayers, and on the simple powerful preaching of Namakei. It was the beginning of a break from centuries of heathen worship. It was the dawning of the day after Aniwa's long dark night.

11

More about Namakei

In the days before the missionary came to Aniwa, when all the people followed their heathen ways, Namakei was a fierce warrior. He was the principal Chief in the whole island, and many a war he had fought in, and many a life he had taken.

When the missionary came, along with Christians from the nearby island of Aneityum, the people of Aniwa thought about killing them. They did not do so, but only because they thought that these visitors would die in any case. For when Paton asked for land to settle on, Namakei and his friends directed the missionary to a particular patch of ground. They called it their 'Sacred Plot'. It was a special part of the island, set apart for their heathen gods. They expected that their gods would kill these strangers for setting foot on that sacred soil. When this would happen they could all share out the blankets, knives, and other things which the missionaries had brought.

But as Namakei and the others watched, the visitors did not die. Day after day they watched, but still Paton and his friends walked about alive and well. Namakei began to wonder if what he had always believed about the gods of Aniwa was really true.

[66]

As Paton laboured to build a house where he and his wife could live on Aniwa, Namakei often walked along to watch what the missionary was doing. One day Paton picked up a smooth piece of wood, took a pencil out of his pocket, and wrote some words on the wood. This he handed to Namakei, asking him to give the piece of wood to Mrs Paton. The dark-skinned old Chief looked at the white man in a strange way.

'But what do you want?' he asked.

'The wood will tell her,' Paton replied.

At this the Chief got angry. 'Who ever heard of wood talking?' he asked. The missionary tried to explain that his wife would read what he had written on the wood, but Namakei could not understand. However, in the end he went to where Mrs Paton was. Imagine his surprise when he saw her just glance at the piece of wood, then set about gathering the tools and nails which Paton had apparently asked for.

When he got back to Mr Paton, he eagerly asked for an explanation of the mystery. How could a piece of wood speak? Paton tried to explain; and as he did so he told Namakei about a book he had never before heard of—the Bible. He explained that in that book God spoke to men, and that if he would learn to read he would then hear God speaking to him too from the pages of the Bible. At this Namakei grew very excited. He came more and more often to where the missionary was working, and helped him learn the Aniwan names for everything. The sooner Missi Paton could speak the language of the island, the sooner he would be able to translate the Bible into Namakei's own language.

For a while this went on. As the missionary laboured to build his house at that spot among the trees, Namakei often visited him. And when the missionary and his wife had tea, Namakei was always pleased to be asked to join them. Then one day Namakei did not come alone. He had a young girl with him— his only child, Litsi. Being the only child of a Chief, Litsi was an important little girl in Aniwa. Why had the old Chief brought Litsi along? 'I want you to train her for Jesus,' he said.

Litsi was a bright girl, and soon began to learn a lot from her white teachers. She had an uncle, a brother of Namakei, who had actually tried to shoot Paton twice. When he saw Litsi dressed so smartly, and coming on so well, he thought he would like his own girl to come with Litsi to the mission house as well. She was called Litsi too; the only difference was that Namakei's daughter was called big Litsi and her cousin was called little Litsi. These young girls, when they went home, told their fathers all about life with the Patons. They spoke of how well they were treated, of how kind the missionaries were. This did more than anything to silence the cruel lies which went around Aniwa, opposing the missionaries' work.

After Namakei had seen Mrs Paton receive a message sent by her husband, written on a piece of wood, he had been eagerly awaiting the time when Mr Paton would translate the word of God into the language of Aniwa. He had given all the help he could to Mr Paton in this work, and now the work of translating some parts of the Bible into Aniwan was complete.

It remained for Paton to set up the type of what was to be the first book ever printed on that South Sea Island. Morning after morning Namakei would go along to where the missionary was working on the old printing press and ask,

'Missi, is it done? Can it speak?'

And one morning Paton was able to answer,

'Yes!'

The old Chief was delighted. 'Make it speak to me, Missi,' he said. 'Let me hear it speak.'

Paton took up the little book and read some verses from it. At this Namakei gave a shout:

'It does speak! It speaks my own language too! Oh give it to me!'

He held the book in his hands, turned it this way and that,

pressed it to his chest, and then a look of disappointment came into his eyes. He closed the book, handed it back to Paton, and said,

'Missi, I cannot make it speak. It will never speak to me.'

Paton tried to explain to him that he had to learn to read before he could understand the message contained in the book. He then looked out a pair of old glasses, because Namakei was peering so closely at the book that it seemed as if his eyesight must be poor. The glasses suited him well, and now he could see the letters clearly on the page.

Paton walked with him to the open ground in the village. He drew the first three letters of the alphabet on the ground, very large, A B C. He then opened the book, showed him these letters on the first page, and left him to search for as many more of these first letters as he could find. It was not long before Namakei was by the missionary's side again.

'I have lifted up A B C,' he announced. 'They are in my head, and I will hold them fast. Give me other three.'

Paton gave him the next three, D E F. Namakei went off and learned up these three letters, and soon was back for more. He was so eager to learn to read that he could not rest—back and fore he had to go, day after day, until he had been taught the whole alphabet. It was not long before he could read, and when people came around he would take out the little book and say, 'Come and I will let you hear how the book speaks our own Aniwan words'.

★

Paton had now lived and worked on Aniwa for about three years. During that time many different things had been blessed by God as a means of bringing some of these islanders to a knowledge of the Lord and Saviour Jesus Christ. The time had now come when these new disciples of Jesus wished to proclaim their conversion to Him.

The Lord's Day, 24th October, 1869, was a wonderful day in the history of Aniwa. After the usual morning service, twelve people stood up before the congregation and were addressed in a special way by Mr Paton. He then asked them if they wished to be baptised, and if they would from that time live as the servants of Christ. The first of the twelve to step forward was their old Chief, Namakei.

After the baptism, the missionary explained to the people the meaning of the Lord's Supper. Then at that Lord's Table sat three white people, six Aneityumese, and twelve from the island of Aniwa. As Paton put the bread and wine into these dark hands, once stretched out to evil and cruel deeds, he felt such joy he hardly knew whether he was in Aniwa or in heaven itself!

★

The last incident in Namakei's life came about like this: There was a meeting to be held on Aneityum which missionaries from different islands in the New Hebrides would attend. There they would report on their work, and discuss what to do in the future. As the days passed, and the time of the meeting drew near, Namakei became more and more eager to attend. In the end Paton agreed to let Namakei come.

As Namakei heard on Aneityum reports of the work of Christ going on on other islands, he was delighted. To Paton he said, 'I am growing tall with joy'.

These meetings on Aneityum went on for some days. At one meeting Namakei was not at Paton's side, and a call came suddenly for Paton to leave the meeting. The call was from Namakei, and when Paton went to him it was to hear him say, 'Missi, I am near to die. I have asked you to come and say farewell . . . Help me to lie down under the shade of that banyan tree.'

Aniwa's missionary helped Aniwa's Chief stagger over to the tree, where Namakei lay down on the leaves and grass. Looking up he whispered, 'I am going. O Missi, let me hear your words rising up in prayer, and then my soul will be strong to go.' Paton could hardly pray; he could not bear to think of parting from his friend, his first Aniwan convert. But amid his tears and sobs, he prayed as best he could.

Old Namakei reached out and took the missionary's hand in his. He pressed it to his heart and said, 'O my Missi, my dear Missi, I go before you, but I will meet you again in the home of Jesus. Goodbye.' After that Paton hardly saw the lifeless form that lay there under the shade of the tree. His thoughts were with Namakei's soul as it entered into glory.

When Paton returned to Aniwa, the old Chief's daughter, Litsi, stood far out on the coral reef to greet the approaching boat. As soon as her voice could carry across the waves, she shouted,

'Missi, where is my father?'

Paton waited till the slow-moving boat drew nearer, then he broke the news: 'He died on Aneityum. He is now with Jesus in glory. This was greeted by a wailing cry, which rose and fell as it was taken up by one after another of the waiting people. Paton was afraid that the Aniwans would in some way blame him for having taken their Chief away, seeing that now he would never return. But the people told him that they had not in fact expected to see their Chief again. When he had left for Aneityum, he had taken farewell of them, telling them that he would sleep at last on Aneityum, and warning them to obey Missi and to help him in the work of the Lord.

The next Lord's Day Paton spoke of their dead Chief to the people. He referred to his conversion, how he lived by faith in Jesus on Aniwa, and died victoriously on Aneityum. Instead of the people being angry they were ready to listen, and thought of the claims of Christ over themselves. And so the death of Namakei was like his sermon on the well. It was used by God to bring his people nearer to his Lord.

12

A Lonely Girl

Eliza Fletcher was not the prettiest of young girls in the south of Scotland about the middle of the last century, but she was one of the liveliest.

Both her parents had died by the time she was about three; after that a rich lady paid to send Eliza to school. She had to send her to quite a number of schools, because usually teachers could not put up with her for very long. In one school Eliza pinned another girl's dress to the tablecloth. When the teacher asked this girl to do something and she got up in a hurry, half the dishes on the table landed on the floor. In another school she jumped down from a window into the grounds and ran away.

One of the places to which Eliza went was called Lochwinnoch. Here she met Maggie and Marjory Smith, daughters of the local minister. There was one difference between Eliza and these two girls; they knew the Lord Jesus as their Saviour, and she did not. However, Maggie and Marjory were full of fun, and the three girls got on together very well.

Then something happened which upset Eliza very much. Maggie fell ill. She had been ill before, but had got better. This time she did not recover.

★

Eliza felt restless. She read books on travel, and then the opportunity arose for her own travels to begin. She applied to take charge of a captain's children when his ship set sail for Australia. She was accepted, so when the *Briseis* sailed for Melbourne in June, 1855, Eliza was aboard.

It was evening when the *Briseis* passed Madeira. The sun, sinking in an orange sky, seemed to cover the mountains of the island with gold. Darkness came on, the stars appeared, and still Eliza sat swinging in her seat in the stern.

About 8 o'clock the weather suddenly changed. The sky became overcast, and the wind began to rise. The other passengers went below, but Eliza stayed on deck. And there she stayed as the storm broke with all its fierceness over that little ship. The waves crashed against the *Briseis'* sides, the foam showing up a creamy colour in the dark. The wind roared through the rigging, and at times the *Briseis* seemed to be going right over. Eliza had to cling on desperately as the deck almost dipped into the sea.

The *Briseis* survived that storm. But she began to leak, and at another stage in the voyage it was thought that she would sink. The uncertainty of life aboard the *Briseis* made Eliza wonder—'what is the most important thing in life for me?' Somewhere on the high seas between England and Australia, tossing up and down in a leaking ship, she felt she found the answer. The greatest desire of the Apostle Paul should be hers as well: *I want to know Christ.*

The trip to Australia and back lasted for eleven months. When the *Briseis* docked at Holyhead, the passengers stepped on to the pier and went their separate ways. For Eliza it was back to Lochwinnoch, and there was one friend there she was especially longing to see again—Marjory Smith.

These were happy days for Eliza. She went for many a walk with Marjory, along the hedgerows of wild roses, or up the hills which overlooked Lochwinnoch. Sometimes she took out her pony and wandered for miles alone across the moors.

But the summer ended, and the time came round for Eliza to leave again. The rich lady who was paying for her education thought that Eliza should now go to study in France. For one last time Eliza and Marjory went for a walk together. Up above Lochwinnoch village they went, until they came to the church-yard. There they stopped and leaned on a white gate leading into a clover field. It was getting dark, but in the light of the moon they could see the white figures of swans on the loch and they could hear them splashing in the water. It was one of the few times that Marjory spoke to Eliza about her need of a Saviour.

'Can you live any longer without God?' she asked. Eliza felt the question go to the bottom of her heart.

The next day Eliza was off for France. She loved travel, and here was a fresh adventure. She was almost a year away, and her stay was broken up by trips here and there. She was happy, she was gay. She was just beginning to think of her return to Scotland when a letter arrived from Lochwinnoch. In it she read that Marjory was very ill. How long the time now seemed, until the holidays would come! But at last they came, and Eliza was back home.

It was August again, and the roses were in full bloom. Each evening, as Eliza walked through the garden to go to Marjory's house, she plucked a rose to leave beside her friend's bed. Before Eliza went back home, Marjory always asked her to read some verses of the Bible with her. One evening Marjory asked Eliza to read John chapter 17. When Eliza came to verse 24, Marjory told her to stop.

'Think of that,' she said. Slowly she repeated the words in which Jesus prayed that His people might be with Him in heaven: 'Father, I will that they also, whom thou hast given me, be with me where I am.'

[75]

Towards the end of the summer Marjory died. Eliza felt very lonely; she had lost her two best friends. She was feeling sad one Friday evening as she went into a church at Lochwinnoch where a meeting was being held. Others came to know Jesus at that meeting, but not Eliza. As she walked away, only the words of the last Psalm sung kept her from despair, *Lord, still Thy mercy lasts.*

She reached home. Then, sitting alone in her room, she took out a pencil and paper and began to write. She was drawing up a list of all the reasons why she could not know Jesus as Maggie and Marjory had done. Her list reached five. Then she thought: These are *your* reasons, but what if God will not receive these reasons when you stand before His Judgment Seat?' She picked up her Bible. God through His word took away all the reasons she had written down. She could not find any reason why she should not be saved.

She went down on her knees in that lonely room and tried to pray. But she found it difficult. She got up again. Now she felt even worse than before. Would God refuse for ever to receive her prayers?

Then she thought of Christ's words, 'Him that cometh to me I will in no wise cast out'. She went down on her knees again, and confessed all her sins. And another verse of the Bible came to her mind and gave her help: 'Surely he hath borne our griefs'. This was a verse which pointed her away from herself and her sins to the Saviour who died on the cross. This, and other verses, directed her to come as a sinner to Christ. And she came; in all her need she came to the Saviour of the lost. She thought, 'When the Judgment Day comes, if I am asked how I came to Christ I will just say that Christ Himself told me, "Him that cometh to me I will in no wise cast out." '

She stayed up very late that night, then she went off to bed. When she awoke next morning, she knew she had a peace she had never wakened to before. As she went around that day the thought kept coming to her mind, 'Lord, I'm nothing but a poor sinner, and yet I'm Thine. And if I'm Thine, I'll be with Thee yet.'

★

It was on a leaking ship, buffeted by a stormy sea, that Eliza had first learned what she most needed in life. It was after the loss of her two best friends that she found what she most needed. And it was in another lonely spot, some time afterwards, that Eliza realized how happy she should now be.

She was in Australia. The weather was so hot that she had to get up at half past five to have her breakfast on the verandah while the air was a little cool. The dew lay heavy on the ground, the kangaroos went hopping past on their way to their feeding-ground, the parrots and the cockatoos were screeching in the branches of the trees. The sky above was one vast dome of blue, without a trace of a cloud. And when darkness fell, the sound of animal life in the Australian bush did not die away. Eliza, lying in her bed, could hear the noise of wallabies moving about, the scream of an opossum, the howl of a distant dingo.

Looking around that part of the Australian outback, Eliza did not see many stately homes. The reason was that her neighbours belonged to Britain, as she did. They did not build beautiful homes out there, because their real homes were in Britain, where they hoped soon to return.

Eliza thought, 'In one way I am like them. Their homes are on the other side of the world, and my home is in heaven. It does not matter very much what life is like in this world; it will not be long before I go to my heavenly home.'

13
Star

India is a land of heat. For months in the year the sky is hard and blue and no rain falls. Dust lies thick over everything, and the trees droop in the heat. The air is like the breath of a furnace.

The main religion of India is called the Hindu religion. The Bible says that there is only one living God, who made us and the world; but in the Hindu religion there are many gods. The people worship these gods by idols—things that they make to represent their gods.

Arulai, the girl in this story, learned to worship idols like the other Indian children with whom she grew up at the beginning of this century. She knelt, she lay on her face before her Hindu idols, she thought of them as her gods.

She liked to ask questions about all kinds of things, but as time passed one question became more important to her than any other. As she looked at her hands and her feet she knew that someone had created them. She ran to her father and asked him, 'Father, who made me?' There were so many gods to be worshipped, but what she wanted to know was, Which of the gods had made her? She asked her father time and again, but he did not seem to know.

Then Arulai had another idea. She would find out for herself which of the gods had made her. She would do this by putting them all to the test in prayer. She was going to ask all the gods which she knew, in turn, if they would change her nature. She had a quick temper, and when she played with other children she sometimes lost her temper; but if she could have her nature changed, perhaps the other children would learn to love her instead of running away. And she thought this: 'The god who can change my nature must be the greatest god of all, and the greatest god must be the god who made me.'

She prayed first to Siva, the god which her family worshipped in a special way. But Siva never answered her prayer. She prayed to other gods whose names she knew, but neither did they answer. She began to feel very lonely. She had been made by Someone; was she to die and never know that Someone who had made her live?

★

There were Christian missionaries in the part of South India where that little girl lived. At the very time when she was spending hours in hopeless prayer they were coming near. They were discouraged; they found it very hard walking through deep burning sand to speak of Jesus in dusty villages where no one seemed to want to listen.

★

It was evening; time for Arulai to go to the outskirts of the town where she lived. The well was there, and it was her turn to fetch water. She came skipping along a well-worn path with her waterpot under her arm.

She stopped. There was a crowd around the well. There were three white people, and some Indians with them. For the moment she forgot why she had come. She stood on the wet stones by the well, and looked and listened as these visitors talked and sang. Then she had seen and heard enough; she began to move away. Suddenly there was a disturbance among the crowd, and she stopped again to watch. But the disturbance soon died down, and she turned again to go. It was then that she heard one sentence, spoken by the Indian preacher, which rooted her to

[79]

the spot. He repeated the sentence several times, although he could not know how much these words meant to her:

'There is a living God. There is a living God. He turned me, a lion, into a lamb.'

Here was Arulai's answer. The question she had asked her father and countless others had been answered by a stranger at the well. This was the God who could change her nature; this must be her Creator. 'He is the living God,' she thought. 'All other gods are dead; Siva is a dead god; I will not worship a dead god any more.' She walked slowly home, but when she went to bed she did not want to sleep. As she said afterwards, 'I wanted to lie awake all night and talk to the living God'.

Next morning Arulai awoke with the joy of her discovery fresh in her mind. Her people had never told her of the living God, and now that she had heard of Him she did not tell them. But she went to hear more about Him from the people whom she had met at the well the evening before. It was against the Hindu religion for her to mix with Christians, but she found the tent where the missionaries were, and squatted quietly on the floor. There were other children there, and although she was shy it was easy for her to sit at the back of the group. She learned a hymn that day. She also heard a little more about the living God who can answer prayer. She did not speak to any of the missionaries, and after a while she slipped out and went home.

She was only a little girl, and she was learning about the living God for the first time. Afterwards God would teach Arulai only to ask for what she knew was according to his will. But for the moment her only concern was, Did He answer prayer? As she made her way home, she thought she would put the living God to the test. She would ask three things from Him, and if He answered two prayers out of three she would be sure He heard and cared for her.

Her mother stood at the door of their house when she got back. She had a stick in her hand. The girl knew that this meant a beating, and in a flash she prayed, 'Living God, O living God! Do not let my mother whip me!' But her mother did whip her. She was angry with her daughter for listening to these Christian missionaries. She thought she could stop her by whipping her and she whipped her till she cried. She cried herself to sleep that night.

Next day she went back with other children to the missionaries' tent; again she squatted at the back of the group. This day she heard about Jesus, and she learned that Jesus was the living God.

As she walked home that night she passed by a tamarind tree whose branches were bending low over the path, laden with ripe fruit. She had been brought up to believe that picking fruit off a tree was stealing; but if the fruit fell to the ground itself she was free to eat it. She prayed to Jesus that some fruit might fall and it fell right at her feet.

It was dark when Arulai reached home that night; she was almost certain to be whipped again. But as she ran along the path she prayed, 'Jesus, living God, don't let my mother whip me!' Her mother met her at the door. She did not whip her.

'I thought you were lost in the dark, my child,' she said, and drew her in.

★

Arulai had a relative who lived near where the missionaries stayed. Her parents allowed her to go and live at this relative's home for the next few weeks. Now she had plenty of opportunities to call at the homes of the missionaries, and to attend their church. She learned more hymns, more about the Bible, more about Jesus, the living God.

But her parents began to hear about all this, and they wanted her back. 'Only for four days,' they said. 'She must come home for a family festival and after four days she can return.'

Arulai suspected nothing, and went gladly. The missionaries, however, watched sadly as she skipped away. They knew that it would be more than four days before they would see that little girl again.

The days became weeks. The anxious missionaries heard nothing at all. Then they heard that she who had said that she was Jesus' child had now denied him. She had been mocked by all her relatives, she had been punished so severely that she had given in. She had gone back to the idols she had left. She had bowed down to Siva again.

The missionaries heard this story. What could they do for her, surrounded as she was by those who did not know her living Lord? They could do nothing, they were told; it was impossible that the girl would ever return. And yet the missionaries could not but wait in hope. They knew that the God in whom that girl had come to trust could do impossible things.

Then, on the morning of one Lord's Day, a missionary was sitting in her room. She was reading the Bible, and many verses seemed to speak to her about Arulai. She read Psalm 86, verse 8, 'Among the gods there is none like unto thee, O Lord'. Arulai had learned the truth of these words for herself. Oh that she who had become Jesus' child would come back to them again!

The bell for morning service began to ring; the missionary would have to get ready for church. Then suddenly the sun-blind was pushed back and Arulai stood just inside the door.

She was very ill. She had been treated in a terrible way. All the family had gathered together against her. They had done everything they could to force her to submit, but she had refused. During the first days of her suffering she had been comforted even by the feel of the Gospel of Mark which she had hidden in her dress. But then they had taken it away. After that she thought:

'They cannot take away Jesus . . . He walked in the fiery furnace with Shadrach, Meshach and Abednego . . . Because He walked with them, the fire could not burn their bodies . . . it could not burn anything on them except their cords . . . It was a good thing that the fire burnt their cords, for if not they could not have walked in the fire with Jesus . . . Lord Jesus, let the fire burn my cords . . .'

'What happened after that?' asked the missionary.

'I don't remember anything,' Arulai replied. 'Only, I think the fire got cool.'

During the next five years her father came many times to take her away. The missionaries could do nothing to force him to let her stay. But every time he appeared one of them slipped away alone to pray. He always left without her. One time he was heard to say, 'What is the matter with me? My hands are strong to take her. It is as if I were bound and held from touching her!'

Arulai had come at a time when the missionaries were very discouraged. They had felt themselves to be walking in the dark. But God had led them to one who was to brighten their path, one whose heart He had prepared to seek Him. And He had

THEY SHALL BE MINE

kept her from denying Him. He had helped her to bear witness to Him in her dark heathen home, and He had brought her back. No wonder the missionaries gave her a special name, and called her *Star*.

14

The Wanderer

Star lived in the hottest part of India, the south east, where the flat land is scorched to a yellowish brown, and the only things which seem to rise up against the heat are the temple towers of the scattered villages.

Poona, where Keshavrao was born, is near India's west coast. It is higher up, the weather is not so hot, and there are more trees. Keshavrao, like Star, was brought up in the Hindu religion. He was told that, if he lived very carefully according to Hindu rules, he might free his soul from sin. The main difference was that, whereas Star's people specially worshipped Siva, Keshavrao's people did not. They devoted themselves to another Hindu god—perhaps Vishnu, Rama or Krishna.

When Keshavrao was twelve years old, he began to wonder about these Hindu gods. He began to think, 'Surely, above all these idols, is a greater God who made all things'. He felt that the best he could do in the service of these idols would not be of any worth in the eyes of the great God, and could not take away his sin.

The Hindu religion teaches that, when we die, we come to this world again in another form. Whether we come in a worse or better form depends on how we have lived. Keshavrao did not want to come back to a worse life than he was living; so, as he grew older, he studied the teaching of his religion to find a way of escape. But then the thought would come to him, 'The great God made everything and gives us everything. Why can He not also forgive our sins, giving us rest and peace?'

Just at that time, Keshavrao met a Christian missionary. He spoke of forgiveness and peace through Jesus Christ, but Keshavrao would not at first believe. 'He is a foreigner,' he thought, 'and his religion if foreign. Surely the great God can be found in India; does he have to use a foreigner and foreign teaching to reveal himself to me?'

He turned from the missionary, but then he met Indian Christians. These were his own people, but they too looked to a foreign Saviour. One of them gave him a book. Here he read of the great God of whom he had thought since he was twelve years old. But still the book spoke of One from outside India as the Way to God; how could Keshavrao believe in Him?

For three months he heard about Jesus and his teachings. Then, one day, as he was out with a Scottish missionary from Poona on a preaching tour, he said to him, 'O Sir, I am determined to be a servant of Jesus Christ'.

When Keshavrao returned from that tour he went to the home he shared with his brother. He told him of the decision he had come to when he had been away. He told his brother how useless it was to worship idols. In fact, he gathered all the little brass idols out of their house and threw them down a well.

His brother was furious. His whole family thought Keshavrao must be out of his mind. He was driven from his home, but his brother followed him with burning hate.

When the next day dawned, Keshavrao went back to the missionary and begged for his protection. But even there his brother followed him, and it was thought better to send Keshavrao away from the area for a time.

So to Bombay he went, and there he met Dr Wilson. He was a missionary in that huge city, and he found employment for Keshavrao at a printing press, connected with the mission which he ran.

After a day or two, Keshavrao also met someone else in Bombay—a Brahman. He was of the strictest and highest order of the Hindus, and when he found out what Keshavrao had done he became very angry. He told Keshavrao he was a fool to think of forsaking the Hindu religion. He told him that the peace he spoke of enjoying through faith in Christ was unreal. If Keshavrao wanted peace, the Brahman said, he should travel to see the sacred places of his own Hindu religion instead of turning to something which had come to India from outside.

The Brahman persuaded Keshavrao to leave Bombay. He put him on a boat that was going to sail for Mangrol, and paid his fare. The point in sailing to Mangrol was that, just inland from the port lay the hill that was sacred for Hindus, called Girnar.

When Keshavrao arrived in Mangrol, he had no money. He found plenty of people who depended on begging to live, and he soon joined them. Together they walked and begged along the coast of Kathiawar.

Among these beggars were many who said that their greatest interest in life was religion. Their strongest fear was, to be reborn in a low state because of sin committed during their lives. To try and overcome their sin and avoid the disaster they dreaded, they would suffer any degree of pain. Some had sat, under the fiercest heat of the burning sun, surrounded by fires. Others had sat with one arm held up in the air until that arm had become withered and useless.

There were also some among Keshavrao's companions who had travelled far. They had been to holy sites, they had bathed in sacred rivers. But as Keshavrao lived with them he knew one

thing: for all the pain they had suffered, for all the sacred places they had seen, they did not have the peace of God in their hearts. And yet for eleven years Keshavrao walked with them. He wore the marks of that group of beggars he had joined; his hair grew long and his face was smeared with ashes.

★

It was in the autumn of 1840 that the cargo ship, the *Wave*, cast off from Liverpool docks. Aboard were a Mr Glasgow and a Mr Kerr—two missionaries who, along with their wives and families, made up the entire passenger list. They were the first missionaries sent out by the Presbyterian Church in Ireland to India. Six months later, they arrived in Bombay.

They worked with Dr Wilson for a time; then they set out for the north, Dr Wilson sailing with them. They passed through fearful storms, and by day the sun beat down on the deck with a scorching heat. At last they arrived at Gogha. When they stepped off the boat it was to stand on earth that had not received rain for nearly two years. The land stretching out before them was a barren dusty brown. Only here and there a green patch could be seen, indicating the presence of a well.

Into that burning land the missionaries went. The travel was slow, by bullock cart, and mostly by night, to avoid the heat. On the eighth day they came to Rajkot.

It was not long before the baby girl belonging to Mr and Mrs Glasgow fell ill and died. A few weeks later Mr Kerr, the other missionary, also became quite ill. He had only been in Kathiawar for ten and a half weeks when he, too, was taken away. Mrs Kerr went home to Ireland; Mr and Mrs Glasgow were left alone.

For a while they continued working at Rajkot; then they felt they should go to the coast for a rest. They would go to Porbandar, and the healthy breezes from the Indian Ocean would bring back their strength. A friend lent them a tent, and the journey to the coast began. Everywhere they stopped on the way, Glasgow used what knowledge of Gujarati he had to speak to the people of their need of Christ. One night a lion came near, but was scared away by the burning lights placed in front of the tent.

At one of the villages where the missionaries stopped, on that journey from Rajkot to Porbandar, they found a beautiful grove of tamarind, pipal and banyan trees. It was eight o'clock in the evening when they arrived, and they pitched their tent for the night in the middle of the grove. They were tired, and the trees gave such welcome shelter from the sun that they decided to spend the next day there as well. Throughout that day crowds came to the tent and Glasgow spoke to them in Gujarati and gave out Gospels to those who could read.

Among the crowds who came that day was one wandering beggar. He told the missionary that he knew other missionaries at Poona; while they talked he agreed that idol worship was wrong and that the Gospels were true. It was Keshavrao.

After some months he came into that missionary's life again. He called at his home in Rajkot and heard more about the way of salvation. He agreed that, whatever he might do, he could not save himself.

Then he was off again, though this time he took with him some books. He called once or twice after that, but it was four years more before he properly came back. The power of the word of God which he had been reading had made him give up the road, and the company of that Hindu beggar sect. This time he had come to stay.

★

For the rest of his life Keshavrao stayed by the missionary, and helped him in his work. He had wandered for years with men who knew nothing about the forgiveness of sins. As he went among his fellow-countrymen now, he made sure that those he

THEY SHALL BE MINE

met heard about it from him. From his years of wanderings he told them no sacred sight they would see, no sufferings they could endure, would take away their sin. Only one Saviour could give wandering sinners peace. The only worthwhile journey was the one He asked all men to make to Him: 'Come unto me, all ye that labour and are heavy laden, and I will give you rest.'

15
Kanousky

'Kanousky, we must run!' Kanousky was a Red Indian boy; he and his mother were in a North American forest. He was only seven years old, but his mother hurried him along as fast as he could go. They ran and ran together until they were so tired they had to lie down on the ground. They spent the night like that, lying on the ground in the open, and did not wake until the next day dawned.

'Mother, why are you crying?'

They were walking through the forest once again, and as they went Kanousky's mother explained to him what had happened. The day before, their tribe had fought with another Red Indian tribe on the bank of a river. Their tribe had lost the battle; Kanousky's father and most of the others in the tribe had been killed. It was a miracle that Kanousky and his mother had escaped.

For days they walked on. They did not know where they were going, but they kept themselves alive by eating the kind of food which Red Indians are good at finding in the forest. One day Kanousky set off after some birds, trying to catch one for food. He tried very hard, but he did not manage it. Then he thought he should go back to where he had left his mother, but he could not find the way. He was lost and alone in a place he did not know. Night came, and, long afterwards, the morning. He tried again to find his mother, but he failed. He ran about from place to place crying out for her, but he never heard his mother's voice in reply.

Days later, some men were working near a wood when they saw a little Red Indian boy. He did not seem to know where he was, nor where he was going. He left the trees and walked over to them. He looked very frightened and sad, and he was asking a question over and over again. But they did not know what he was saying; he spoke in a language they did not understand.

These men were kind to Kanousky. They gave him some food, and they brought him to the farmer for whom they worked. He, too, was kind to Kanousky, and gave him clothes and food. Kanousky stayed with the farmer, and after some time he began to go out with the other farm workers when they went to work in the fields. He was glad to have something to do, but he was very lonely. He thought of his mother many times a day. He often remembered that spot where he had last seen her in the wood; he longed and longed that he would see her again.

★

One of the farmer's servants was called Joseph. Once a year this servant saddled up his horse and set out for a town fifty miles away. He stayed there for a fortnight or so, attending to business for his master. Some time after Kanousky arrived at the farm, the time came round when Joseph had to make this trip. He asked the farmer if Kanousky could go with him, and the farmer agreed.

The sights which Kanousky saw in the town were very strange to him. He saw shops, and he enjoyed gazing at the different things the shops had on display. One day he was wandering about the town when he began to hear the sound of people singing. He made his way to where the sound was coming from, and found himself standing in front of a large house. A man was just about to go in, so Kanousky asked him, 'What for they make that noise in that big house?'

'They are praising God in that house,' the man replied.

'Praising God! What is that?' Kanousky asked again.

'Come in and see,' said the stranger. So Kanousky went in with him.

What Kanousky saw and heard in that church was all new to him. He heard the people singing, then he saw a man get up at the front and begin to speak. He talked and talked and talked. One thing he said many times; he had read it out of a book before beginning to speak: 'We must all appear at the judgement seat of Christ'.

When Kanousky got out of the church, there was one thing in his mind. He had to get back to Joseph to tell him what he had seen and heard, and to ask him what he thought about it all. Joseph wasn't interested, but Kanousky kept asking him about God, of whom the man at the church had spoken so much. At last Joseph said, 'God made you and all the world'.

'God made me and all the world!' Kanousky repeated. 'I never heard that before.'

Soon Joseph and Kanousky had to pack up and begin the journey home. They took many things back with them, but one thing which Kanousky took back meant more to him than anything else. It was the memory of what he had heard in the church. He kept thinking of death; he felt that he was a sinner, and that he was not ready to die. His friends noticed a change and tried to cheer him up. When he told them what was worrying him they replied that he was not a sinner; they said that he did not need to think about these things.

One night, as Kanousky lay awake in bed, a part of that sermon he had heard came back into his mind. It was the part in which the preacher had spoken about the mercy of God. There and then Kanousky prayed for the first time in his life,

'God have mercy on me. I do not see You, but You see and hear me. God have mercy on me.'

That was a prayer which he repeated often, not during that night only, but also throughout the months that lay ahead.

At last the time came round when Joseph was to return to the town. Kanousky asked if he could go with Joseph again, and his master said, Yes, he could go. In town, when God's Day came, Kanousky made his way to the church he had been in the year before.

Near the beginning of the service, the minister prayed. He asked God to give to those who were troubled a peace which none could take away. Kanousky's heart was so troubled that he thought that the minister must have been praying for him alone. 'That's me,' he said out loud, and some people in the church turned to look at him. The sermon was on what Jesus said, 'Him that cometh to me I will in no wise cast out'.

Their stay in town this time lasted for a month. During that time the children in the house where Kanousky stayed taught him the letters of the alphabet. And when he rode out of town with Joseph, he had a Bible and some leaflets in his luggage; Kanousky had begun to read.

One beautiful summer's evening, back at the farm, Kanousky was sitting outside. His day's work was done, and as usual he was reading his Bible. He was in a quiet spot, in the middle of a clump of fir trees. That night he read about the death of Jesus on the cross. Kanousky cried when he thought of the sufferings of the Son of God; especially he felt sorry because it was for the sins of people like himself that Jesus died. But he was happy too; for he believed the words which Jesus spoke to sinners, 'Him that cometh to me I will in no wise cast out'.

Then trouble started between Kanousky and some of the other farm servants. These men did not care about God, and yet they spoke about Him. When they were angry they would use His Name in a wrong way. Kanousky felt that he had to speak to them about it. This made the other servants angry, and they complained to their master. The farmer did not want to do anything against Kanousky, but these men said that, if Kanousky was not sent away, then they themselves would go. So the farmer told Kanousky that he must leave. In a day or two Kanousky left, a little money in his pocket, his possessions tied in a bundle on his back.

When he had walked some distance away, he turned to look at the farm again. He was a boy of seventeen years now, but he began to cry. That farm had been his only home since he had lost his mother in the wood; his only friends were there. And then he thought, 'No, you have your best Friend with you; Jesus is with you still'. He walked on for the rest of that day, and as the darkness came down he found a spot among some trees where he could sleep.

It was the afternoon of the next day when he reached town. He went to the house where the children had taught him to read. He was welcomed into the house, and was allowed to stay there until he could get work. One man who attended the church heard about him, and gave him work on a farm just outside the town.

Kanousky was happy in his new work, but he often thought about his old master. One day, when Joseph was in town, Kanousky heard from him that his old master was ill. Kanousky was very sad; he felt that his old master was not ready to die. So when Joseph went back to the farm, Kanousky rode at his side.

Kanousky found the farmer sick with a fever from which some of the farm workers had already died.

'You see me very weak,' the farmer said, 'but I am hoping to get better soon.'

'I hope so, too,' Kanousky replied.

'Kanousky,' the sick farmer said, 'you look sad. Is anything the matter?'

After a while Kanousky answered, 'I think, if you get a little worse, you would die; and then, where would you go?'

'To Heaven, I hope.'

'So I hope,' said Kanousky, 'but . . .'; and he tried to explain some things which he himself had learned. He told the farmer that only by the blood of Jesus could anyone go to Heaven; that if he did not have his sins forgiven for Jesus' sake, he could not go there.

'Well,' the farmer said, 'I am too ill to talk just now. You must come back in the evening.'

In the evening the poor man's mind wandered from one thing to another, and Kanousky could not say much to him. However he had plenty of opportunities to speak to him after that, for the farmer's nurse became ill and Kanousky himself nursed his old master night and day. And when Kanousky at last left the farm once more, he felt that his visit had been used by God to do some good. The farmer had been healed of the fever which had almost killed his body. But Kanousky could also hope that his old master had been healed of the disease of sin which had almost destroyed his soul.

★

Three months after that, a wealthy lady visited the town. She had an Indian lady servant with her. On the Lord's Day, both these visitors went to Kanousky's church. Along with Kanousky and the others who believed in Jesus, they sat at the Lord's Table; Christ's death was being remembered in the church that day. After the service, the minister asked Kanousky along to his house. The two lady visitors were also asked to come.

The visiting lady was with the minister and his family in the living room upstairs. The lady's servant and the minister's servant were in the kitchen with Kanousky. Suddenly there was a

CHRISTIANITY COMES TO KOREA

piercing scream from the kitchen. The people in the living room rushed out and down the stairs to see what had happened. They found that the lady's servant had collapsed in shock to the floor. The minister's servant was bending over her, and Kanousky was standing by. Tears of joy were streaming down his face, as he said again and again, 'Blessed God! Blessed God!'

'What's the matter?' asked the minister.

His servant seemed unable to speak for a moment or two, then he explained, 'He has found his mother, and she has found her son.'

16
Christianity Comes to Korea

Korea is a beautiful country, lying between Japan and China. The ground bears all kinds of crops, and from the mountains you see many a breath-taking view. In the wild parts of North Korea you might meet some black bears: in Central and South Korea you might catch a glimpse of a tiger.

★

In 1832 a man from Germany came in a boat to the West Coast of Korea. He was really sent by a trading company to see if trade could be opened up with this fertile land, but he had with him piles of Scriptures as well. While he was waiting to hear whether or not the Koreans would allow trade to begin,

[97]

he gave out Bibles and tracts. As he went about doing this he found that, in Korea, true Christianity was quite unknown.

The Koreans did have strong views about how people should behave towards one another. But did they worship God? Not really! They had a great respect for the past, and they showed this in their worship of the spirits of those who had died.

The Koreans did not allow trade to begin, and in the years that followed they made it quite clear that they wanted the rest of the world to leave them well alone. No more Scriptures went into Korea for thirty-three years. Then Robert Thomas, a Welsh missionary to China, met two Koreans there. He soon became convinced that God was calling him to bring the Scriptures to the Korean people. He decided this, even though all foreigners were threatened with death if they crossed over and stood on Korean soil.

Robert Thomas was wondering what to do when he heard about *The General Sherman*. She was an American ship, going on a voyage of exploration to Korea. The missionary asked for permission to travel from China to Korea on this ship, and was accepted. So on board he came, armed with his tracts and Bibles, and *The General Sherman* set off. They sailed across the Yellow Sea, and arrived on the West Coast of Korea. They followed the coastline until they came to the mouth of the broad Tai Tong River, and then sailed up this river. Now and again they stopped, and every time Mr Thomas gave out copies of the Scriptures, or left them on the river bank.

The ship moved on slowly inland, and soon they were in sight of the old walled city of Pyengyang. By this time it was clear that they were no longer welcome, and the visitors decided that they would have to leave. They turned *The General Sherman* round and began to sail away, but the water was lower now than when they had come up the river and the boat ran aground. The Koreans watching on the river bank knew that the visitors were trapped. The passengers and crew of *The General Sherman* knew it too, and they abandoned ship. As they struggled to the water's edge and clambered up the bank they all tried to defend themselves. All of them, that is, except one. For as the Koreans closed around Robert Thomas they saw that he held neither sword nor pistol in his hand. He was carrying a load of books, and all he did with the last few seconds of his life was to throw these books to the crowd, or to thrust them into the hands of his killers.

★

Years passed, and Korea became more friendly towards foreigners. Some of the Bibles which Mr Thomas had given out along the banks of the Tai Tong River had been read in secret at first; but now they were being studied openly. More Bibles had also been sent, and some of these were changing the hearts of the Koreans within the walled city of Pyengyang itself. Then other missionaries came, and a Christian church began.

One of the missionaries who came to Korea from America at the beginning of the century was called Dr Blair. He was asked to work among the cities to the north of Pyengyang. So along these country roads he went—rough tracks which wandered through rice fields or climbed up steep and rocky mountains. At night time he would sleep in an inn. Korean travellers, sometimes many of them, would be sharing the main room with him. The air would get very hot from the kitchen fire at one end; it might also get very thick with smoke from the long pipes of the Korean men. But here Dr Blair would have to sleep as best he could.

In the morning he might choose a road leading to where he knew a market was to be held that day. Now and then he would have to leave the track to make way for an enormous ox which a man was leading with a load to the market. From a hill-top he would see the track zig-zagging down the mountain side, and winding along the valley floor to where the market was to be. At one point he could pick out a woman with a pile of cloth on her head. At another he could see a man carrying a load of firewood or of eggs. And there, turning a corner by a rock, was a boy leading a donkey laden with rice. Dr Blair would begin his descent, and soon he would overtake a few people. Surprise and pleasure would show on their faces as they heard the American speak their language. Then Dr Blair would begin to speak to one particular man in the group. They would talk together of all kinds of things and then the missionary would ask one special question.

'Have you ever heard the story of Jesus?'

'I have heard something,' the man would reply, 'but not very much.' So on they would walk along that stony road, and Dr Blair would speak about Jesus to this Korean man. Perhaps they would get so interested in their conversation that they would

[100]

both stop, stand aside, and let the others going to the market pass them by. Perhaps the man would be in church the next Lord's Day. In this and in other ways, the Korean Church spread as the years went by, and grew strong.

17
Choo Kichul

Yasu Kyo.

It was a sign hanging outside a small straw-thatched house in a city of North Korea. What did the words mean? *The Church of Jesus.*

That was not the only sign of its kind in Korea. Not many years of this century had passed before there were a large number of them, hanging outside buildings up and down Korea. Some of the buildings were large, some small, some were in the country, some in cities. But inside all of them Koreans gathered who had come to believe in the Lord Jesus Christ.

The government of Korea, however, did nothing to encourage them. Actually the land was now in the hands of the Japanese, who had gone to war with Russia, and much of the fighting had been done on Korean soil. After the defeat of Russia, Japanese troops had simply stayed on in Korea and now the country was ruled by Japan. As time went by, the Japanese began to enforce their own religion on the Koreans. Part of this religion involved worshipping the Emperor of Japan as if he were God, and of course no Christian could feel free to join in such a thing. God sometimes calls his people to suffer for His sake; this was one of those times in the history of the Korean Church.

Choo Kichul was born in Oongchun, just before the time when Dr Blair arrived in Korea. Choo went to a Christian school in North Korea, then to College, and lastly he went to study in Pyengyang.

When he had finished his training as a minister, Choo preached at one or two smaller churches in South Korea, then he was called to a large church in the city of Pyengyang. This was the city, you will remember, below which *The General Sherman* ran aground and near which Robert Thomas had died as he gave out Bibles to his killers.

From the beginning, Choo told his congregation not to obey the government's orders to worship as the Japanese did. However, for some time he was free to teach and preach as he thought right. Then, in 1938, he was arrested. For six months he was kept in prison, but they were not altogether unhappy months for Choo. He had his Bible with him, and he spent his time reading it. Especially did he read those verses which speak of how God is with those who have to suffer for His sake.

It was a day of great joy for the congregation of Sanchunghyun Church, Pyengyang, when their pastor was released. Now he was free to preach again, but what was he going to say? If he were to preach against the Japanese worship he would be put in prison again. Would it be better to say nothing about it at all? Choo prayed to God for wisdom to know what to do. After that he felt quite sure of his duty. In August, 1939, he went into the pulpit of his church, and told the people that without any doubt it was a sin to do as the Japanese government required them to do. As usual, there were spies in the church that day, and they told what Choo had said. He was arrested again.

It was hard to leave his home this second time. His blind old mother asked where he was going, and why he was leaving

her. His children cried. But Choo's wife showed great faith in God. When he had gone, she joined the rest of the believers in praying for her husband. They did not ask so much that he might be released, but more that God would strengthen Him in prison to obey His will.

Then the government organised a special meeting at Choo's church. It was announced that Choo was no longer the minister there, and that another minister was to be appointed instead. But the congregation would not even listen to this. Instead they sang, over and over again:

> *A mighty fortress is our God,*
> *A bulwark never failing,*

[103]

Our helper He, amid the flood
Of mortal ills prevailing . . .

They sang so loudly that they drowned the voices of those who spoke for the government. They did not want a minister who would be more obedient to men than to God. And in any case, Choo was their minister still, even though he was in prison again. All through those months, even in the cold and dark of winter mornings, they met at 5 o'clock to pray for him.

Choo suffered a great deal while in prison the second time. But he had the comfort that another Christian man was in the same cell with him. This man afterwards said that Choo would often pray, in his pain and weakness, 'Lord, don't leave this weak Choo Kichul too long, but hurry up and take him away'.

His second period in prison lasted for six years. But all the time his congregation prayed for him, his wife visited him, and God was with him to give him strength and joy. Then, on April 12th, 1944, he said, 'I'm going, but what of the Sanchunghyun sheep? I'm going to the Lord.' To his wife he said, 'I've gone the road I'm supposed to go. Follow in my steps. Let us meet in Heaven.' The next day his soul went to begin an eternity of freedom in the service of his Heavenly Lord.

18

The Girl No One Knew Was There

Outside a house in a poor street to the north-east of London stood an old type of wheel chair. Called a spinal carriage, it was a large, awkward thing with high sides, great big wheels, and handles at one end.

Inside the spinal carriage lay a little girl called Nellie Marriott. When only a baby of 11 months, doctors had discovered that she had a serious illness; since then she had been an invalid. Now she lay flat on her back, her body encased in a 'still jacket'. Even her legs, arms and head were strapped down. She suffered great pain; especially her back, her left hip and left leg were often in agony; and she had the most fearful headaches.

Nellie's father was a soldier in the Territorial Army. He had a large T on his cap, which stood for *Territorial*. But one day he came to Nellie and told her that he was going off to join the regular army. It was 1914, and war had begun. He would be away for a long time.

Before he left, Nellie's father asked her to try to cheer up her mother while he would be away. Then he took the T from the front of his cap, and sewed it on to her teddy bear. The T stood for *Teddy* now, and it also reminded Nellie of what her father had asked her to do while he was away.

In the years that followed, the war was often in Nellie's thoughts. She heard war planes flying low overhead, and she used to worry about them. She had to be rubbed every night with methylated spirits, and she used to hear her mother warn her sister not to put the bottle of methylated spirits near the fire in case it would explode. Nellie used to be afraid that a spark would fall down from one of these planes and set her back alight. But the planes did not bring fear every time they came into her life. Once a fighter plane crashed nearby, and as the pilot walked up her street he saw her. He didn't say, 'Oh! you poor dear' (Nellie hated people saying that). He bent down over the high sides of her carriage and kissed her. She was absolutely thrilled.

Whenever the neighbours saw Nellie's spinal carriage outside, they could be sure that *Spot* was not far away. He belonged to a neighbour, actually, but he was almost Nellie's dog. A bull terrier, he was not at all good looking; but he sat beside Nellie's carriage faithfully, day after day. If ever she needed help she had only to tell that dog and help would be on its way.

Because of Nellie's illness, she was not being taught to read. No one even read her stories; the doctors thought that it would not be good for her as it might excite her brain. She did not know the first thing about the Bible.

★

Sometimes Nellie's mother would feel very tired. She felt like that one Lord's Day, and she thought she would have to rest. Nellie's sister Molly used to go to a Sunday School at a church hall nearby. For once, Molly's mother asked her to take Nellie with her to the hall so that her mother could have peace to rest. So Molly wheeled Nellie's carriage out of the house, along the road, and up to the church. When they got inside Molly pushed the carriage behind a row of chairs at the back of the hall, and left Nellie there alone. No one seemed to notice she was there.

By the time that Molly's class finished, she had forgotten about Nellie altogether. She walked straight out of the hall and went with another girl along to her house. Nellie was only six and a half years old, but she was used to lying quietly for hours. There was nothing she could do just then, she felt, but lie and wait. Perhaps Molly would come back in a little while.

She stared up at the ceiling, and wondered what was going on now in the hall. She could hear voices from the other end, and the noise of chairs being arranged. Then the hall grew quieter, and a man began to speak.

'I'm going to tell you about words which Jesus spoke from the cross,' Nellie heard him say: *'It is finished'*. First he explained what was finished—God's plan of salvation for sinners. Nellie had never heard one word of this before. Next, he went on to say why there was a need for salvation; that man had sinned against God. Then the speaker lowered his voice.

'He must be speaking to the younger children at the front just now,' Nellie thought. The man said,

'None of you can say that you are so young you have not sinned.'

'Yes,' Nellie thought, 'I have had wrong thoughts. I have sometimes been angry at Molly, because she can go out and wear pretty clothes, when I have to lie at home and only wear a nighty which has been split down the back.'

The speaker went on to show that it was only through the death of Jesus, the sinless Son of God, that sinners can be saved. He quoted the words in which Jesus spoke of his death on the cross, 'I, if I be lifted up from the earth, will draw all men to me'. How he emphasised the word *all!* Nellie began to wonder, 'Perhaps that *all* includes me'.

Then he went on to speak about Christ being nailed to the cross. He spoke about the pain, and he said,

'Pain was just as much to him as it is to you.' Nellie thought of all the pain she had suffered the night before, and she began to cry. She was not crying for herself, but for this Saviour, Jesus. She knew that, if she had any choice, she would be free from all pain. But Jesus had chosen to suffer, and even to die, for sinners like herself! Lying on her carriage, hidden at the back behind the chairs, Nellie Marriott received the Lord Jesus as her Saviour. She hadn't even known His name before that day. But as she lay there hearing the word of God, she knew her sins had been forgiven for His sake. And now it was as if He was there Himself, His arms around her bed. She had often wept before, because of the pain. This was the first time that she wept for joy.

Molly meantime had left her friend's house and had made her way back home. When she came in the door without Nellie, her mother jumped up in alarm.

'Where's Nellie?' she asked. Then Molly remembered,
'I left her at the church.' Her mother was out of the door in
a flash, and ran along to the church. The meeting had ended,
and those in charge of the church had begun to lock up. They
had just discovered Nellie, and were wondering what to do with
her, when her mother arrived.

In those days, Nellie was in and out of hospital all the time.
The day following, Monday, she began one of her spells in hospital. Nurses lifted her off her carriage, placed her on a flat board
and fastened her arms, her legs and her head.

In the same ward as Nellie was a young boy. John was ten
years old, and he was very ill. He was crying all the time, and

he asked for his bed to be pushed over so that he could be near to Nellie. The doctor said that it might help John to stop crying, so the nurses pushed his bed over.

Nellie couldn't do anything like holding out her hand, but she could speak to John. The first thing she had to do was to get him to stop crying. Then she said,

'John, there's Someone here who can do something better than making your pain go away for a little time.'

'Oh, tell me!' John cried. 'I want to get rid of this pain.'

Then Nellie told him about Jesus. She had only heard about Jesus herself the day before, but she could remember a lot of what she had heard. Then John interrupted.

'Stop a minute, girl,' he said. 'You've always been good, I expect. I've been a very naughty boy before I was ill. I don't think God would want me.'

'Oh! but it was for wicked people Jesus died,' Nellie replied. 'If we feel we have no sin then Jesus has no place for us, because it's for sinners He died.'

Soon after that the nurses separated Nellie and John. It was less than an hour later that he was to die. The nurse was washing John when she noticed that he had got much weaker. She heard him saying something, and she bent down to listen.

'Lord Jesus of that little girl,' he was saying, 'be my Saviour too.'

Later that week, when Nellie was still in hospital, there was one night which was especially difficult. Nellie felt terrible pain, but at the same time she felt the Lord Jesus very near. Then,

'Nellie, do you love me?' He seemed to say to her.

'Yes,' replied Nellie within herself, 'Lord Jesus, I love you very much.'

'Well,' Nellie felt Jesus' reply came back, 'I have work for you to do when you grow up.' From that moment, Nellie was sure that she would yet walk.

The next afternoon there was a visiting hour, and Nellie's mother came up to the hospital. As Mrs. Marriott was walking along the corridor leading to Nellie's room, the doctor met her. They began talking about Nellie in hushed voices, thinking she could not hear. But Nellie knew what was happening; although her sight was poor, her hearing was very good. The doctor was explaining to Mrs. Marriott just how ill Nellie was. He said that she should not be raised up on any account; if she were, she might die.

'Her condition is so bad,' the doctor went on, 'she might go at any time. She certainly will never walk, and I don't think she will ever grow up.' Nellie wanted to shout out from her room,

'You silly man, I am going to grow up and work for Jesus,' but she was able to keep quiet. She heard her mother beginning to cry, and then she heard the doctor saying,

'Now, Mrs. Marriott, pull yourself together. If she knows what I've told you, she will go all the quicker.'

When her mother came into Nellie's room, she tried to hide her tears. She talked about different things, and did not speak about what the doctor had just said. Suddenly Nellie told her,

'Mummy, I am going to work for Jesus when I grow up.'

★

That happened in 1917. Now, in 1981, Nellie Marriott still lives just outside London.

In the years between, she has had many troubles. Her house was bombed during the second world war, and she was unconscious for three months. Apart from the tuberculosis she had as a child, she has suffered pain throughout her life from other causes as well. But as she looks back to her childhood she does not think of her troubles, nor of her constant pain. These years are full of sweet memories. Especially she is thankful for God's so helping her that what she said to her mother in that hospital ward came true. She grew up, she did walk, and she *did* work for the Lord.

Of the many things God helped her do, which is she most grateful to remember? *The Bible classes she ran for hosts of London children during the second world war.* It's not surprising, really. It was at a meeting for young people that she herself first met the Lord—though no one knew she was there.

19
Phru Chik

Some people climb up high mountains just for the fun of it, or to see a wonderful view from the top.

This story is taken from the life of a man who climbed to one of the highest countries in the world. Why did he do it? Not just for fun, not just to see the view, but to bring good news to the Balti people who lived there. These people are not without religion. Like other Moslem people, the belief of the Balti is: 'There is no God but Allah, and Muhammad is his prophet'. Jock Purves climbed with others up to the country where the Baltis live to tell them of Jesus Christ.

For days on end they climbed up into the mountains. Sometimes they passed through valleys covered with trees, where mountain bears could be seen. At other times they walked across flat land where no trees could grow, land where the snow was often very deep. They were high up, but looking above them they could see mountain peaks rising higher still. Up, up, the steep white slopes soared into the cold blue sky. At last the party began to descend again to a level where people could live. There, in the lonely mountains of Lesser Tibet, they found the Balti people. Having once reached them, the missionaries knew that they were now almost cut off from the rest of the world.

The houses in which the Baltis lived were very low, and the roofs were flat. Usually there was a wood fire burning in the middle of the floor, and no outlet for the smoke! The natives were used to it, but the smoke got into the visitor's eyes. So, if they went to tend the sick or to take out teeth, they had to make their visits very short!

As well as caring for the sick, the missionaries began a school for Balti boys. The pupils did not have exercise books and pencils, as you have at your school. But they had wooden boards, coated with a white substance found in the mountains, and on this they wrote with pointed sticks, dipped in dark-coloured clay.

As the pupils learned to read, Jock Purves began to give them lessons in which they read the Bible. These lessons would go well, until a boy would come across words in his reading passage which spoke of Jesus as the Son of God. You will remember that the Balti people believe in Muhammad as Allah's prophet, and not in Jesus Christ the Son of God. So when a Balti boy came across a Bible verse which spoke of 'Jesus Christ, the Son of God' he would not read out these words. Jock Purves would ask the next boy to read the verse, but when he came to 'Jesus Christ, the Son of God', he too would stop. And so it would go on right round the class. Sometimes the boys would get so upset at being asked to read these words that they would all come to Jock Purves after school and tell him they were going away. And they would; but he would go after them to their villages and speak to them, and day by day a few would return to school until all were back again.

Phru Chik was one of the pupils in Jock Purves' Bible Class. The Balti people were poor, and Phru Chik must have come from one of the poorest homes. He was always dressed in rags. But he was a clever boy and a good reader. He had a big head and a bright smile. Apart from this, there was nothing special about Phru Chik. Like the other boys he had always refused to speak about Jesus Christ as the Son of God.

Then, one day, it was Phru Chik's turn to read a verse which spoke of Jesus Christ as the Son of God. He stood up and read the verse right through. The other boys wondered if they had heard correctly. Did they not all believe in Muhammad as Allah's prophet, and did they not all reject this Christ with equal hatred? But they had heard all right. They had heard Phru Chik read words which spoke of Jesus as the Son of God. They stared at him. After a moment he looked round at them and said. 'You need not be surprised. I can read these words now. I have Jesus Christ in my heart.'

THEY SHALL BE MINE

There were not many, but there were a few others who also
came to know the Lord Jesus Christ among those Balti pupils
in that far-away school. It was good that Jock Purves and his
friends went when they did: it was good that Phru Chik and
the others came to have Jesus in their hearts before it was too
late. Not long after that school was started, a flood from melting
snow swept through that valley, high in the mountains of Tibet,
and carried the school away.

20

Franco Maggiotto

Mamma, l'acqua come può correre senza gambe?

He was a little Italian boy, aged two and a half. He lay face
down on the bank of a stream, watching the water running by.
His mother had told him many times not to go near the stream,
but Franco could not resist the temptation to return. Now she
was coming from their nearby home, and he could see that she
was going to smack him. But he was only concerned to find
an answer to the question with which this story began:

'Mummy, how can the water run without legs?'

Franco was born in the city of Turin, in Northern Italy, in
the summer of 1937. He was not very old when he had to leave
the streets where he had played, and the stream which he had
often visited. For war broke out, and his father, who was in
the Italian army, arranged for Franco's mother and their children

to leave Turin. Soldiers came and carried them up into the mountains to hide. Not long after they had left that house, it was blown up by a bomb.

The war ended in 1945, and after that things became more normal again. Franco could settle down to his work at school. But there was one thing which unsettled him. Italy is a Roman Catholic country and the priests and nuns of that Church have a great influence in the Italian schools. For many hours in the week Franco had to learn about the Church. He was taught that it is not possible for anyone to be saved outside the Roman Catholic Church. He was taught that he had to confess his sins to a priest, and that, if he did not do so, terrible things would happen to him.

When he was ten years old, a priest told a story which frightened Franco. The story was about a boy who did not confess all his sins to a priest. During the night, as he lay in bed in his school dormitory, a black goat with burning eyes came and licked this boy's hands and face. In the end, according to the story, the other boys in the dormitory asked a saint of the Roman Catholic Church to help. He came with a cross and drove the goat away. But the boy who had not confessed all his sins to the priest had been burnt to a cinder. This story, of course, was not true. The priest told it to Franco and his friends because he wanted them to be afraid of the Church, and to feel that if they disobeyed anything that the Church taught, they would suffer severely for it. The story certainly had an effect on Franco. For years, he was afraid that the goat in that story would come at night to lick his hands or face. He even got up at night to put a chair against his bedroom door to keep the goat away.

Not that everything was gloomy and unhappy in Franco's boyhood days! He got on well at school. Once the teacher offered a prize to the boy who could best repeat a poem in Latin. Another boy learned the poem so well that he could say it perfectly. But Franco went one better. He learned that Latin poem so well that he could repeat it perfectly, backwards! He got the prize.

★

When Franco was still a teenager, he began to feel a deep desire to know God. He asked a priest for advice about what he should do. The priest said that Franco must do something to overcome the sin which was within him. He advised him to go to a monastery: that is, a place in which a man can live apart from the world, spending his time in prayer to God. Why do men go there? Because they hope that, by doing this, they will please God; that by living such a life they will overcome the power of sin in their hearts.

When Franco heard of the monastery on Monte Corona he decided that that was the one to which he would like to go. This monastery is built on one of the seven hills of Rome. The walls around it are so high that the monastery seems almost like a city itself. There are vast grounds within the monastery, and if you walk there you can look down on the old city of Rome. You can even see the Vatican and the palace of the pope, the head of the Roman Catholic Church.

Franco found life in the monastery very hard. Along with the other monks he had to wear one garment of thick white wool. In the summer it was far too hot, in the winter he shivered with cold. The monks were not allowed to eat any meat, and they could not talk to anyone except the priest, to whom they were to confess their sins. Franco had not been there a year before he became ill. A doctor came to see him and said that he was not fit to cope with this hard monastic life.

Did Franco know God any better after being in that lonely monastery? No! However, he now thought that, if he could serve the Church as a priest, going out among the people and teaching them, perhaps this would be a help to himself. So he left the monastery and began to train to become a parish priest.

The Italian Riviera is a lovely stretch of coastline. Many people go there for holidays, because the weather is warm and there are miles of beaches where they can bathe in the Mediterranean Sea. Franco did not have to take a holiday to see the Italian Riviera. He was sent there by the Roman Catholic Church after he had finished his training to become a priest. So he came to Ceriale in Liguria. He was still a young man, but the other priest above him in the parish was old. Franco had to work extra hard, and he got to know the people in his parish well. They became very fond of him. And when the time came for Franco to move to another parish the people of Ceriale were not at all pleased.

But he had to leave them, for he had been told by those above him in the Roman Catholic Church to go to Imperia. This is the capital town in the province of the same name. Most of the houses in that town are built closely together, but at the top of the hill in the centre of the town there is a clear space. Built in the middle of that space and rising up to overlook the whole town, is a huge church. The church is given that position so that people will see how very important it is. And soon Franco was not an ordinary priest, serving in that church; he became higher than a priest, and had four priests who served under him. Franco's father, who lived in the province of Imperia, used to lead a group of his soldiers into that grand church. And who would be in charge of the service? Franco! How proud his family were that he was becoming so important.

But was he really getting on so well? Franco had sought for God at Monte Corona. He had left there and come to Ceriale: and now he had left Ceriale for Imperia. But was he now any nearer to God? At Ceriale he had begun to read the New Testament. At Imperia he had started meetings with students, in which they all studied the word of God together. Franco was still searching, he was looking desperately for God. He did not know Him yet, but as he read the Bible more and more he began to realise one thing—the Roman Catholic Church and the Bible did not agree. The Church of which he was a priest said many things which he could not find in the Scriptures, the word of God. He would have to choose between the Bible and the Roman Catholic Church. As time passed Franco became more and more conscious of this: if he was to find God, it would be in the Bible that he would find Him.

Sometimes he stayed all night in that great church. When the caretaker came in the morning he would find Franco lying in front of the altar. He had been trying to pray all night, but he had fallen down exhausted and gone to sleep.

Before I tell you how Franco's search ended, I must explain to you about the Mass. The Mass is the Roman Catholic communion service. At the communion service in the Protestant Church we have bread and wine, reminding us of the body and blood of Christ, and pointing us to His death. But Roman Catholics believe that, at the Mass, the bread and wine are actually changed by the priest into the body and blood of Christ. The priest then holds up the bread and wine to God, as if he were offering up Christ Himself.

One day Franco was in charge of the service at his church. The church was filled with people, and he was walking up the steps before the altar to perform the Mass. As he did so a young student was reading a passage from the Bible. The passage was Hebrews chapter 10. Listening to that passage, standing there before the altar, Franco suddenly understood two things. He saw that it was wrong for him or any other priest to say that he could offer Christ again to God, when Christ Himself had done this once for all. And he also understood that here, in the very words of Scripture, was what he had been looking for all those long years. He saw that God, in sending His own Son to the death of the cross, had provided the only means by which

man's sin can be washed away. All the suffering that Franco had endured at Monte Corona and afterwards had been a waste of time. Even if he could endure sufferings many times greater than these, they would never bring him near to God. The only way to peace was through the sufferings which Christ had already endured on the cross, long, long before.

The other priests looked at him. They did not know what was wrong. What was happening to Franco? He turned to them by the altar and tried to explain what he had just come to know:

'What are we doing here? Christ has done it all on the cross of Calvary.' But they did not understand. They led him out of the main part of the church and up the stairs. They told the people that Franco was not feeling well and concluded the Mass themselves.

After that, Franco could never perform the Mass again. He remained in the Roman Catholic Church for a time, but before very long he was put out. He still did not know anybody in any other church. But God provided for him and led him to Holland and then to England. And now he is back in Italy, telling his people what he learned for himself: that God makes Himself known through His word and that we can know peace with Him only through the death of His Son on the cross of Calvary.

21
The Baron's Grandson

Sicily is the largest island in the Mediterranean Sea. Shaped like a triangle, it lies between the south of Italy and North Africa.

The land of Sicily is mountainous, the mountains rising to their highest peak in Mt. Etna. For most of the year, if you glanced up at Mt. Etna, you would think it very cold because it is capped with snow. But sometimes the mountain erupts, pouring out fire and smoke and molten rock. Mt. Etna is a volcano. Once the lava rose 766 metres into the air and in 1928 the town of Mascali was completely destroyed. On that occasion, and on several others, people living close to Mt. Etna have been killed. It is a wonder that anyone lives on Sicily! But then, it is their home; their people have lived there for centuries, and where else would they go?

Pietro Lorefice's people were Sicilians, born and bred. His grandfather was a baron of the old town of Modica, seventy miles south of Mt. Etna. It was in Modica that Pietro was born on the 17th of February, 1938.

Pietro's parents wanted him to serve the Roman Catholic Church. So when Pietro reached 14 years of age they sent him to a special training school.

The school lay to the south of Modica, at Ispica. Pietro was taken through the town to the far side, where he saw two large buildings on one piece of ground. At the entrance was a sign inscribed on stone, *Collegio Serafico dell' Immacolata.* This was the name of one of the buildings—a school where boys were trained to become friars of the Roman Catholic Church. Here Pietro was to stay for the next three years.

Life in the school was hard. At times the boys were not allowed to speak to anyone. But at least they could sometimes go out and roam around the school grounds. From there, Pietro could see Cape Passero, the southern corner of Sicily, reaching out into the blue waters of the Mediterranean.

One day, Pietro was working in the school garden. He saw a booklet lying on the ground and picked it up. On the front cover he read, *Evangelo di Giovanni*—Gospel of John. Pietro was very interested and he read some pages of the booklet. But when he showed it to some others in the school there was a great outcry. The teachers were very angry. They wanted to know how the Gospel had come to be within the school grounds. They asked all the pupils, but none of them knew; or, at least, none of them would say. This Gospel did not have the stamp of the pope's approval; it was therefore burnt by the school head in the presence of all the boys. But as Pietro saw the Gospel he had found go up in flames he thought, 'I would like to get another Gospel to keep'.

As Pietro studied in that school, he often thought of the building which lay next door. It was a convent where friars stayed. If Pietro continued his training, he would one day live the same kind of life as these friars were living beside him. Little by little, he learned how these friars lived.

Each friar had a small room to himself, with bare white walls. He spent his time praying and reciting words, and from a window in one wall a supervisor could look in to see if he was doing this or not. Every Friday these friars had to think about their sins in a special way. They had to recite Psalms in which they confessed their sins, while lashing themselves with whips at the same time.

Pietro worked at his studies for three years. Then, one day, he found someone in the school doing something wrong. There was a great fuss about it and Pietro was involved because he had seen what was done. What especially upset Pietro was that he had discovered something like this in a place where people were supposed to be living in a way that was pleasing to God. In the end he left the school. So he never entered that convent; his training to become a friar stopped.

He kept on studying, however, at an ordinary school. A few months after he had left the school at Ispica, he travelled to Milan to attend a students' conference. Milan is in the north of Italy, and Sicily is in the south, so it was quite a long journey to have to make by train.

Opposite Pietro in the train compartment was a man who sat during the journey with a book open on his knees. The book was a Bible. Pietro had never seen a Bible before, and he could not hide his interest from the man who was reading it. Soon they began to talk about the Bible. The man asked Pietro questions which he could not answer. So Pietro thought, 'This man was not trained as I was, yet he knows more about these things than I do!'

This experience made Pietro even more determined to find a Bible for himself. But it was not so easy. The Roman Catholic Church did not encourage its people to read the Bible, and Pietro found it very difficult to get one.

Some months after this, back in Sicily, Pietro was talking one day with his school friends when one of them said to him, 'If you want a Bible, I have one at my house. My father got one when he was in America in 1939, and when he came back he took it home with him.' Pietro did not need to be asked twice; the next day he held a complete Bible in his hands for the first time in his life.

He read the Old Testament. He came on to the Gospels,

and read the life of Christ. Then he read the Epistles, which explain the meaning of Christ's death.

The days passed, and God taught Pietro as he read His word. He showed him that he should not just accept what other men taught him about how to worship. He also taught Pietro that he could not please God by anything that he could do himself.

There was one epistle which Pietro grew to like especially. It was written by Peter, the apostle with the same name as himself. In the second chapter of I Peter, Pietro read about Christ as the rock on which the church of God is built. He saw that Christ alone could be his Saviour, and he trusted in Him. So the words about Jesus, written by one Peter long ago, became true for another Peter too in modern times: 'Unto you therefore which believe he is precious'.

Pietro's family were different. They trusted in the Roman Catholic Church to tell them what to believe. They did not think it right that Pietro should read the Bible as he did—why could he not just accept what the Church said, as they did? They tried to persuade him to change his mind, but how could he deny what he had now discovered to be true? Every day things got worse; in the end he had to leave his family altogether.

Where could he stay? On the outskirts of Modica he found a place dug out of the rocks. The sides of the rocks made walls, and there was an entrance to this rough room which could be closed. Water trickled down the rocks, making the place very damp. But there was a bench where Pietro could sleep at night, using his school books as a pillow. When he combed his hair in the morning before going to school, he used as a mirror the lid of a shoe polish tin! It was an unusual life for the grandson of a baron of Modica.

Pietro did not want to give up studying, so he was glad to get part-time work as a salesman. With the pay from this job he managed to pay for his food, his clothes and his books.

After almost a year, Pietro's family allowed him to rejoin them.

Of course, while accepting him, they tried again to bring him back to the Roman Catholic Church. One aunt even promised him a new red sports car if he would come back. But he had found more than a sports car in the Bible which so offended them.

Now finished at school, Pietro wanted to serve the Saviour whom he had found in the Bible, but what training did he have? A Bible School in Switzerland heard of him and offered him two years of training free, if he would help in the work of the school office. He accepted the offer gladly, and when he had finished that course he went down to Naples to work with a pastor there.

He was near Sicily again, but not near enough! After six months in Naples he crossed over to his native island and settled at Ragusa, capital of the province in which he had been born.

Pietro worked at Ragusa for ten years, gathering people together to study the Bible and to hear the gospel preached. He was still at Ragusa when a serious earthquake shook western Sicily in 1968. News came to Ragusa that several villages had been destroyed, that many people had been left injured and homeless.

One member of Pietro's group in Ragusa had a bus. Pietro and some friends filled that bus with food and other things, and off to the stricken area they went. They passed to and fro among the tents of the homeless, till all the things they had brought were given away. As well as bringing food and other help, Pietro also brought the word of God to these needy people. He began to travel every fortnight from Ragusa to hold meetings, and then one day a young mother with two girls came to speak to him. She told him that, through these meetings, she had come to know Jesus as her Saviour.

That was his first encouragement, and as he kept visiting the area he began to feel that God was leading him to work there. So Pietro left Ragusa and settled in Ribera, near where the earthquake had been. God blessed his work, and today Pietro has three churches to look after around Ribera.

If you ever visit Sicily, perhaps you will call to see Pietro and his wife Teresa. And if you learn a little Italian you can also talk with their four children, Rosalia, Paola, Susanna and Romualda.

Sources

The main sources used are listed below, numbered according to the chapters in the book to which they relate. This list could provide a guide to further reading, though many of these books are now out of print.

1 Reports of the Mission at Pesth appearing in issues of *Sunday at Home* in November, 1866 and April, 1867. *Memoir of John Duncan* by David Brown.

2 *Noted Ministers of the Northern Highlands* by Donald Beaton.

3 *Religious Life in Ross* by John Noble.

4 *Some of the Great Preachers of Wales* by Owen Jones; *Echoes from the Welsh Hills* by David Davies.

5 Details obtained directly from Franco Maggiotto.

6 Same as for chapter 4, with *John Elias, Life, Letters and Essays* by Edward Morgan.

7 *Christian Leaders of the 18th Century* by J. C. Ryle.

8–11 *John G. Paton, Missionary to the New Hebrides,* ed. by James Paton.

12 *Memorials of Eliza Fletcher* by C. A. Salmond.

13 *Overweights of Joy* by Amy Wilson-Carmichael.

14 *The Tiger Tamed* by R. H. Boyd.

15 *Kanousky* by J. Van Zweden.

16–17 *Korean Pentecost* by William Blair and Bruce Hunt.

18 The outline of Miss Marriott's story was taken from a tape distributed by the *Torch Trust For The Blind,* Torch House,

Hallaton, Market Harborough, Leics. Further details were given by Miss Marriott during correspondence by tape and letter. It may be of interest for some readers to know that copies of a tape by Miss Marriott can be purchased from *Falcon AVA, Falcon Court, 32 Fleet Street, London EC4Y IDB.* The title of the tape is *Facing Incurable Illness.*

19   *The Unlisted Legion* by Jock Purves.

20   *Dr Kidd of Aberdeen* by James Stark.

21   Details obtained directly from Pietro Lorefice.